KitchenAid

Immersion Blender
Soup Cookbook

Table of Content

Introduction to the "KitchenAid Immersion Blender Soup Cookbook: 365 Days of KitchenAid Hand Blender Soup Recipes Including Fruit, Spicy, Thai, Creamy, Chicken, Vegetable and Seafood Soup"

Soup has been a beloved culinary staple across cultures for centuries, and rightfully so. Not only does it offer a comforting and satisfying meal, but it also packs a nutritional punch. Soups are an excellent way to incorporate various wholesome ingredients, such as vegetables, lean proteins, and nutrient-dense broths, into your diet.

One of the soup's primary benefits is its ability to hydrate the body. Soups are typically composed of a liquid base, making them ideal for increasing fluid intake, which is essential for optimal bodily function. Additionally, depending on the ingredients used, soups can be a valuable source of fiber, vitamins, and minerals.

When it comes to creating velvety, smooth, and flavorful soups, a KitchenAid immersion blender is an invaluable tool. These handheld blenders allow you to effortlessly puree ingredients directly in the cooking pot or container, eliminating the need for transferring hot liquids to a separate blender. This saves time and effort and reduces the risk of spills and mess.

KitchenAid immersion blenders are designed with powerful motors and sharp blades, ensuring that even the toughest ingredients are blended to the desired consistency. These versatile blenders can handle everything from silky smooth bisques to chunky vegetable soups. Many models also feature variable speed settings, allowing you to control the blending process and precisely achieve the desired texture.

This comprehensive cookbook is a gem for soup enthusiasts and those looking to incorporate more homemade, nutritious soups into their diets. With over 365 recipes, this book offers a year's worth of delicious and diverse soup options, catering to various dietary preferences and flavor profiles.

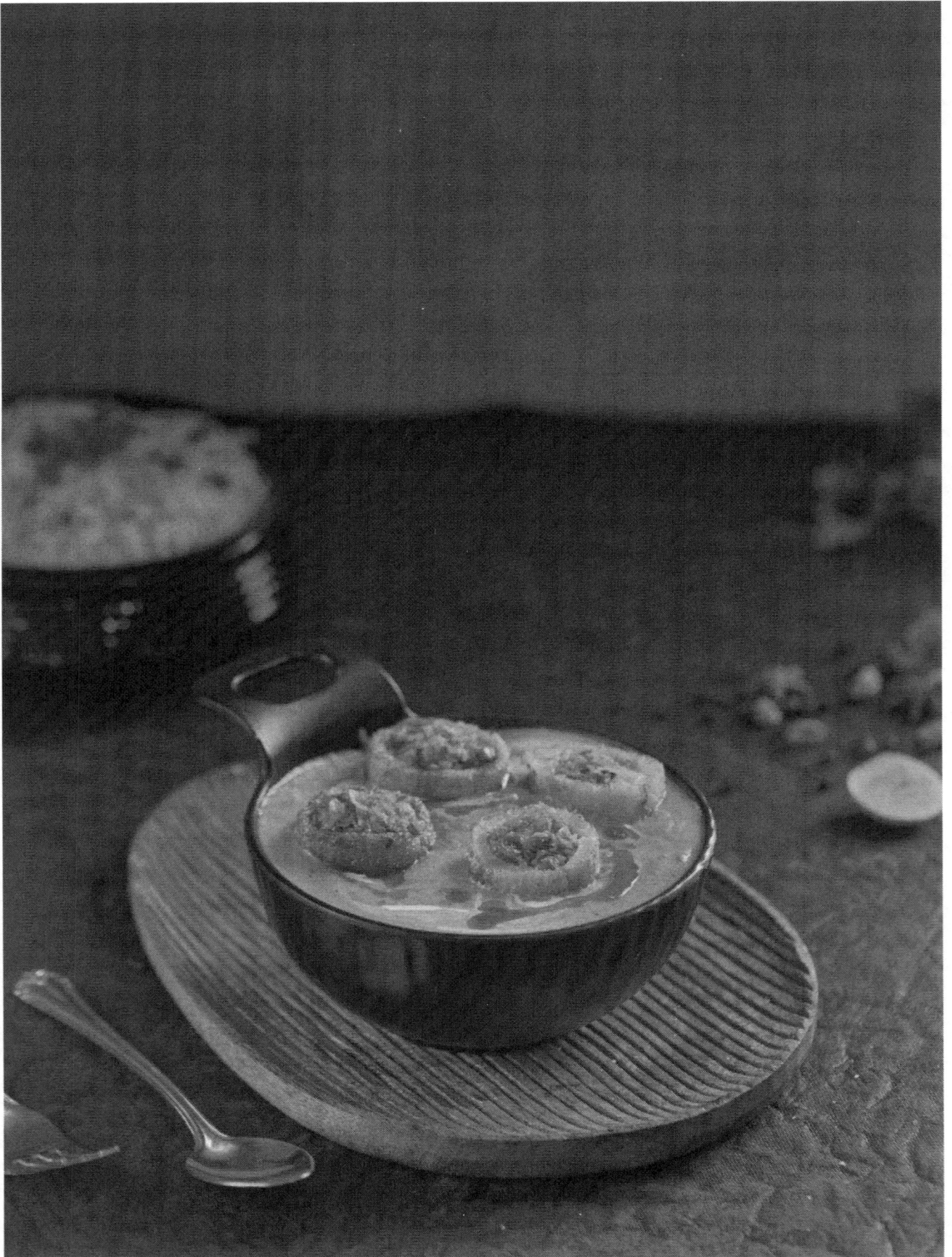

The Chapters Are Thoughtfully Organized, Covering A Wide Range Of Soup Categories

Fruit Soup: Explore the refreshing and unique flavors of fruit-based soups, perfect for warm weather or as a delightful palate cleanser.

Spicy Soup: Ignite your taste buds with a collection of bold and fiery soup recipes that are sure to satisfy your craving for heat.

Thai & Curry Soup: Immerse yourself in the aromatic and exotic flavors of Thai and curry-infused soups, offering a delightful fusion of spices and herbs.

Creamy & Bisque Soups: Indulge in the velvety smoothness of rich and creamy soups, ranging from classic bisques to decadent purees.

Chicken & Meat Soup: Explore hearty and comforting soups featuring tender chicken or meat, perfect for satisfying appetites.

Roasted Soup: Discover the depth of flavor that roasting vegetables can bring to soups, creating a unique and robust taste experience.

Protein Based Soup: Fuel your body with nutrient-dense, protein-packed soups that are both filling and flavorful.

Green Vegetable Soup: Embrace the vibrant flavors and health benefits of green vegetables in a variety of delicious soup recipes.

Root Vegetable Soup: Celebrate the earthy and comforting flavors of root vegetables in soups that are perfect for cooler weather.

Seafood Soup: Savor the rich and diverse flavors of the sea with a myriad of seafood-based soup recipes that are sure to delight.

Whether you're a seasoned soup enthusiast or just starting to explore the world of homemade soups, this cookbook is an essential addition to your culinary library. With its diverse range of recipes and the versatility of the KitchenAid immersion blender, you'll be able to effortlessly create restaurant-quality soups in the comfort of your own kitchen.

Imagine the satisfaction of serving a warm, homemade bowl of soup to your loved ones, knowing that it's not only delicious but also packed with nutritious ingredients. This book empowers you to experiment with flavors, textures, and cultural influences, allowing you to embark on a culinary journey around the world, one soup at a time.

Embrace the convenience, versatility, and health benefits that this cookbook and a KitchenAid immersion blender have to offer. Elevate your soup game and tantalize your taste buds with an array of flavorful and nourishing soups that will undoubtedly become family favorites.

About KitchenAid Immersion Blender:

KitchenAid immersion blenders, also known as hand blenders or stick blenders, are versatile kitchen tools designed for convenient and efficient blending tasks. These handheld appliances are known for their durability, powerful motors, and ergonomic designs that make blending tasks a breeze.

One of the standout features of KitchenAid immersion blenders is their removable blending arms, typically made of high-quality stainless steel. These arms are equipped with multi-point blades that can effortlessly blend, puree, and emulsify a wide range of ingredients directly in pots, bowls, or containers. This eliminates the need for transferring hot liquids to a separate blender, reducing mess and saving time.

KitchenAid immersion blenders offer variable speed settings, allowing users to have precise control over the blending process. This feature enables users to achieve the desired consistency for various recipes, from chunky salsas to velvety smooth soups and sauces. The ergonomic handles and lightweight designs make these blenders comfortable to hold and operate, even during extended blending sessions.

In addition to their blending capabilities, KitchenAid immersion blenders often come with additional attachments and accessories, such as whisks, choppers, and frothers. These accessories expand the functionality of the blenders, allowing users to whip cream, chop nuts, or froth milk for beverages.

KitchenAid immersion blenders are designed with user safety in mind, featuring non-slip grips and secure locking mechanisms to prevent accidental detachment during use. Many models are also dishwasher-safe, making clean-up a breeze.

The Benefit of Using KitchenAid Immersion Blender

Using a KitchenAid immersion blender offers several benefits that make it a valuable addition to any kitchen:

Convenience: Immersion blenders allow you to blend ingredients directly in the cooking vessel, eliminating the need to transfer hot liquids to a separate blender. This not only saves time but also reduces the risk of spills and mess

Versatility: KitchenAid immersion blenders can be used for a wide range of tasks, such as pureeing soups, making smoothies, emulsifying sauces, blending batters, and whipping cream or dressings. Their powerful motors and sharp blades ensure efficient blending and smooth results

Space-saving design: Immersion blenders are compact and take up minimal counter space compared to traditional blenders. They can be easily stored in a drawer or cabinet when not in use, making them a great choice for small kitchens or those with limited storage space.

Easy cleaning: Many KitchenAid immersion blenders have removable blending arms that can be detached for thorough cleaning. Some models are even dishwasher-safe, further simplifying the cleaning process.

Precise control: KitchenAid immersion blenders often feature variable speed settings, allowing you to adjust the blending intensity for different tasks. This level of control ensures you can achieve the desired texture, whether you want a smooth puree or a chunkier consistency.

Ergonomic design: KitchenAid immersion blenders are designed with ergonomic handles and non-slip grips, ensuring a comfortable and secure grip during use, even for extended blending sessions.

Additional attachments: Some KitchenAid immersion blender models come with additional attachments, such as whisks or choppers, expanding their functionality and allowing you to perform multiple tasks with a single appliance.

By utilizing a KitchenAid immersion blender, you can streamline your cooking and food preparation processes, saving time and effort while enjoying the benefits of a versatile and convenient kitchen tool.

FRUIT SOUP

1. MANGO SOUP

Prep Time: 15 Minutes | Cook Time: 30 Minutes

Total Time: 45 Minutes | Serving: 4

Ingredients

- 1 cup of diced mangoes or 1 cup of diced papaya
- 1/2 tsp ground coriander
- 1 tsp curry powder, to taste
- Salt
- 1 tbsp peanut oil
- 3 cups of stock
- 1/2 tbsp freshly grated ginger
- 1/2 cup of sliced yellow onion
- 1/4 tsp ground red pepper (adjust according to desired spice level) or 1 small jalapeno, finely minced
- 1 1/2 cups of yams, peeled and cut into 1/2-inch cubes
- 1 tbsp butter or 1 tbsp ghee
- Chopped cilantro leaf (for garnish)

Instructions

1. Over medium heat, melt the peanut oil and butter or ghee in a big stock pot. Add chopped onions and cook until soft.
2. Add the fresh ginger, coriander, red pepper, and curry powder. Stir just until the spices are mixed in.
3. After adding the stock, bring to a boil. After that, put in the mango and yams. Put the lid on top and turn down the heat. Cook for 30 minutes or until the yams are soft enough to poke with a fork. Add the salt, and if you need to, taste to see if the seasoning is right.

4. With the KitchenAid immersion blender, you can blend half or all of the soup until it's the consistency you want.
5. Add some chopped cilantro leaves as a garnish.

2. STRAWBERRY SOUP

Total Time: 5 Minutes | Serving: 5

Ingredients

- 1 cup of vanilla yogurt
- 2 pounds strawberries (approx. 2 ¾ pints)
- 1 tbsp lemon juice
- 1/4 tsp ground ginger
- 1/2 cup of orange juice
- 3 -4 tbsp sugar
- 1/2 tsp vanilla
- 1/4 tsp ground cinnamon
- ⅓ -1/2 cup of coconut cream from a can of full-fat coconut milk, optional

Garnish (optional):

- orange zest
- whipped cream
- mint

Instructions

1. Put everything into a KitchenAid Immersion blender and chop it up first, then blend it until it's smooth. If you want the soup to be thicker, add more yogurt. If you want it to be thinner, add more orange juice with an extra pinch of sugar.
2. You can serve the soup right away, but it tastes even better after being chilled for at least two hours. Before serving, taste it and add more sugar if you like. After being chilled, the sugar tends to become less sweet.
3. Add the garnish you want.

3. CHILLED AVOCADO CUCUMBER SOUP

Prep Time: 10 Minutes | Cook Time: 10 Minutes

Total Time: 20 Minutes | Serving: 4

Ingredients

- 3 stalks of scallion chopped
- 1 tsp salt
- Ghee or butter for frying
- 2 large or 3 medium Haas avocado
- 1/2 small cucumber peeled and seeded
- 1-quart chicken stock
- 2 tbsp fresh lemon juice
- 1 leek chopped
- 1/2 cup of coconut milk (optional)
- 1 tsp minced fresh parsley for garnish

Instructions

1. Melt the butter or ghee in a pan and cook the leek until soft.
2. It will smell good for a minute after you add the scallions and garlic.
3. Warm the soup in the quart pot until it's barely thick.
4. Take the soup off the heat and add the vegetables that have been sautéed.
5. Using the KitchenAid immersion blender, blend the avocado, cucumber, lemon juice, and salt in a pot until the mixture is smooth.
6. If it seems thick, you can add some water.
7. Put it in the fridge and serve it cold with coconut cream and parsley.

4. JACKFRUIT SOUP

Prep Time: 5 Minutes | Cook Time: 20 Minutes

Total Time: 25 Minutes | Serving: 4

Ingredients

- 5g dry oregano
- 75ml olive oil
- 2g cayenne pepper (powder)
- 10g fresh basil
- 1,5 liters of vegetable stock
- 5g fresh sage
- Pinch of salt & black pepper
- 500g Naked Jack - raw jackfruit chunks

Instructions

1. Boil the jackfruit chunks in the vegetable stock for 15 to 20 minutes until soft. Make sure the Naked Jack is no longer frozen.
2. After adding the olive oil and spices, leave the soup alone for a few minutes.
3. Use a KitchenAid immersion blender and blend it until it's smooth and creamy.
4. Your soup is ready to be served after you add as much salt and cayenne pepper as you

5. PLUM SOUP

Prep Time: 5 Minutes | Cook Time: 20 Minutes

Total Time: 25 Minutes | Serving: 4

Ingredients

- 1 1/2 lbs red or black plums, cut in half and pitted
- 1 tsp tarragon leaves
- 1 cup of apple juice
- 1/4 tsp Kosher salt
- 1 tbsp ginger, peeled and sliced into chunks
- 1 cinnamon stick
- 1 tbsp agave
- Yogurt, for serving

//Instructions

1. Combine plums, apple juice, ginger, cinnamon sticks, tarragon agave, and salt in a pot. When it starts to boil, lid and reduce the heat. Let the plums cook for 20 minutes or until they are very soft. Throw away the cinnamon stick.
2. Blend the mixture with a KitchenAid immersion blender until it is smooth.
3. Put it in a container in the fridge for about an hour or until it's cold. Put it in bowls and top with yogurt before serving.

6. PUMPKIN COCONUT SOUP

Prep Time: 10 Minutes | Cook Time: 25 Minutes

Total Time: 35 Minutes | Serving: 4

Ingredients

For the soup:

- 1 29-ounce can of pumpkin puree
- 1 1/2 tsp salt
- 2 tsp minced garlic
- 1 tbsp brown sugar
- 1 tsp ginger paste
- 1 tbsp olive oil
- 4 cups of chicken broth
- 1 can of coconut milk
- 2 medium gold potatoes peeled
- 1 medium onion diced
- 1 tsp cumin

|**For topping:**

- crumbled bacon
- chopped cilantro
- heavy cream
- toasted pumpkin seeds

Instructions

1. Put the olive oil in a big pot on medium heat. Add the onion to the pot and cook it until it gets soft. Put the ginger and garlic in the pot and cook until they smell good. Put the potatoes, chicken broth, coconut milk, salt, cumin, brown sugar, and pumpkin puree in the pot. Bring the soup to a slow boil. Leave it there for 15 to 20 minutes or until the potatoes are soft. A KitchenAid immersion blender should be used to puree the soup. The lid should be left open so that steam can escape. Serve hot with any toppings you like.

7. CHILI-LIME BLACK BEAN SOUP

Prep Time: 15 Minutes | Cook Time: 24 Minutes

Total Time: 39 Minutes | Serving: 6

Ingredients

- 1/2 tsp ground cumin
- 1 tsp kosher salt
- 1 1/2 tsp dried oregano
- 1/4 cup of chopped cilantro
- 1/4 cup of chopped scallions
- 3 tbsp plain low-fat Greek yogurt
- 1 medium jalapeño pepper, seeded and minced
- 1 large onion, chopped
- 2 cups of reduced-sodium chicken broth
- 1 tbsp jarred minced garlic
- 2 tbsp fresh lime juice (Juice of 1 lime)
- 1/8 tsp cayenne pepper
- 60 ounces canned black beans, rinsed and drained
- 1 tbsp extra-virgin olive oil
- 1 tsp ancho chili powder

Instructions

1. Heat the oil in a big nonstick soup pot over medium heat. Add the onion, jalapeño, garlic, and salt. Cook, stirring now and then, for about five to ten minutes until the onions are soft. Mix in the cayenne, oregano, cumin, and chili powder. Cook for one minute while stirring. Put the beans and broth in the pot and turn the heat high. Turn down the heat and let it simmer, uncovered, for about 10 minutes. Add lemon juice to it and stir.

2. Take the pot off the heat and use a KitchenAid immersion blender to puree the soup. Add 1/2 tbsp of yogurt to each bowl and top with scallions and cilantro to serve. About 1 cup of food is made per serving.

8. SPICY SWEET POTATO KALE CANNELLINI SOUP

Prep Time: 25 Minutes | Cook Time: 40 Minutes

Total Time: 1 Hour 5 Minutes | Serving: 12

Ingredients

- 3 garlic cloves, minced
- 3 cups of chopped fresh kale
- 2 tbsp olive oil
- 1 tsp honey
- 1/2 tsp salt
- 3 cans (14-1/2 ounces each) vegetable broth
- 1 tsp rubbed sage
- 2 medium Granny Smith apples, peeled and chopped
- 1/2 cup of heavy whipping cream
- 3/4 to 1 tsp crushed red pepper flakes
- 1/4 tsp pepper
- 2 cans (15 ounces each) of cannellini beans, rinsed and drained
- 1 medium onion, finely chopped
- 3 pounds sweet potatoes (about 5 medium), cubed
- Optional toppings: Olive oil, giardiniera, and shredded Parmesan cheese

Instructions

1. Put oil in a 6-quart stockpot and heat it over medium-high heat. Stir the onion in and cook for 6 to 8 minutes until soft. Put the garlic and cook for one more minute. Add the apples, honey, spices, and broth, and mix them in. Bring up the temperature. Lower the warm and allow the potatoes to cook for 25 to 30 minutes with the lid on.
2. Use a KitchenAid immersion blender to blend the soup. Then, add the soup back to the pan. Add the beans and kale. Cook over medium heat, uncovered, for ten to fifteen minutes, stirring occasionally until the kale is soft. Add the cream and stir. Put on top of your choice of toppings.

9. SPICY CHICKEN SOUP

Prep Time: 15 Minutes | Cook Time: 50 Minutes

Total Time: 1 Hour 5 Minutes | Serving: 6

Ingredients

- 1 Cup of Chopped Carrots
- 1 tbsp Extra Virgin Olive Oil
- 2-4 Cloves of Garlic, Minced
- 1 Cup of Chopped Celery
- 29 Ounces Cannellini Beans
- 1 Sweet Onion, Diced
- 32 Ounces of Chicken Broth
- 1 Pound Chicken Breast
- 1 tsp Salt
- ¾ Cup of Buffalo Sauce.

Instructions

1. Put minced garlic and chopped onions in the bottom of the big soup pot with olive oil to start. On medium heat, cook the onions until clear.
2. After that, add the chicken breast, broth, buffalo sauce, and salt. Mix everything and put the lid on the pot. For 30 minutes, simmer on medium to low heat.
3. Take the chicken breast out of the pot and put it in a mixing bowl. Use a hand mixer to shred the chicken.
4. Then, make a thick, creamy broth with a KitchenAid immersion blender.
5. Last, add the chicken that has been shredded back in, along with the carrots and celery. Let it cook on low heat for 20 minutes or until the vegetables are soft. Hot food!

10. SPICY BUFFALO CHICKEN SOUP

Prep Time: 15 Minutes | Cook Time: 40 Minutes

Total Time: 55 Minutes | Serving: 4

Ingredients

- 750ml chicken stock
- 1 cup of diced carrots
- 1 small white onion (chopped)
- 1 tsp sea salt (add additional sea salt to taste)
- 2 garlic cloves (minced)
- 1 rotisserie chicken (shredded)
- 1/2 cup of hot sauce of choice
- 5 cups of Taylor Farms Diced Cauliflower
- 1 cup of diced celery
- Cracked black pepper, to taste
- 1 tbsp extra virgin olive oil
- Fresh cilantro for garnish
- Sliced avocado for garnish
- Chopped green onions for garnish

Instructions

1. Put olive oil in a big pot. Set the stove to low heat. Add the onion, carrots, celery, and garlic when the olive oil gets hot and bubbles. Sauté for 10 minutes or until the onion turns transparent.
2. Put in the cauliflower, hot sauce, chicken stock, and salt and pepper. Then, put the lid on top. For about 30 minutes, or until the cauliflower is soft, cook on low to medium heat.
3. Put the soup on low heat and remove the lid. Then, use a KitchenAid immersion blender to blend the soup until it is smooth.
4. Every few minutes, stir in the shredded chicken.
5. Feel free to add more salt or pepper if you like.
6. Put soup into bowls for each person and top with green onions, cilantro, and sliced avocado.

11. SPICY TAHINI MUSHROOM SOUP

Prep Time: 12 Minutes | Cook Time: 40 Minutes

Total Time: 52 Minutes | Serving: 4

Ingredients

- 3 packages of assorted mushrooms
- 1 tsp fresh thyme
- 2 chopped celery stalks
- 1 chopped onion
- 2 chopped garlic cloves
- 2 tbsp Soom Premium Tahini
- 1 tbsp flour
- ½ tbsp Sriracha
- 2 tbsp olive oil
- Salt and pepper to taste
- 3½ cups of vegetable stock

Instructions

1. Warm the olive oil on medium-high heat. Add the garlic, onion, and celery stalks, and cook them until they are soft. Stir in the flour until it's well mixed in.
2. Put fresh thyme and mushrooms in it. Stir-fry until everything is completely cooked.
3. Tahini, Sriracha, and vegetable stock should be added. Put the lid on top and cook for 40 minutes. Mix using a KitchenAid immersion blender. Put in as much salt and pepper as you like.

12. SPICY PUMPKIN SOUP

Prep Time: 10 Minutes | Cook Time: 20 Minutes

Total Time: 30 Minutes | Serving: 3

Ingredients

Spicy Pumpkin Soup:

- 3 Garlic Cloves
- ½ tbsp pepper
- 1 tbsp Cumin
- 1 tbsp Light Butter
- ½ Yellow Onion
- ½ tbsp Salt
- 2 ½ Cups of Vegetable Broth

- 1/2 tsp Smoked Paprika
- ½ Cup of Light Coconut Milk
- ½ tsp Turmeric
- 1 tbsp Chili Powder
- 1 tsp Sugar
- 3 Cups of Pumpkin Purée

Instructions

1. Cut the onion and garlic cloves up. Put away.
2. Put the big pot on medium heat and add the butter.
3. When the butter is melted, put the onion in it and cook it for 3 minutes until it turns transparent.
4. Put in the garlic and cook for one minute.
5. Pepper, chili powder, cumin, turmeric, and salt should be added. For three minutes, stir and cook.
6. Put in the pumpkin, coconut milk, and vegetable broth.
7. Bring it to a boil, then let it cook for 5 minutes.
8. To puree the soup, move it to a KitchenAid immersion blender. Blend until smooth.
9. Add the soup back to the pot.
10. For 10 minutes, keep the heat low.

13. SPICY TOMATO SOUP

Prep Time: 15 Minutes | Cook Time: 30 Minutes

Total Time: 45 Minutes | Serving: 4

Ingredients

- 1 pound cherry tomatoes or grape tomatoes
- ½ cup of vegetable broth or chicken broth
- ¼ cup of basil leaves
- ½ tsp red pepper flakes
- 1 tbsp olive oil
- ½ tsp sea salt
- 2 cloves of garlic smashed

Instructions

1. Warm the oven up to 400°F. Add the garlic cloves and whole tomatoes to a tbsp of olive oil and toss them around. Then, add a lot of salt.
2. Put the tomatoes in the oven for 25 to 30 minutes or until some burst and blister. Take it out of the oven and let it cool a bit.
3. Put the tomatoes and their juices into the KitchenAid immersion blender. Blend until the texture you want is reached.
4. Put the soup in a saucepan and set it over medium-low heat. Put in basil leaves. Bring to a low boil, then cook for 10 to 15 minutes.
5. Take out the wilted basil leaves, or use an immersion blender to blend the basil into the soup right in the pot.
6. Serve with toast, crackers, or a hot grilled cheese.

14. SPICED LENTIL SOUP

Prep Time: 20 Minutes | Cook Time: 35 Minutes

Total Time: 55 Minutes | Serving: 8

Ingredients

- 1 tsp Turmeric
- 8 ounce Red Lentils (about 1 1/4 cups)
- 1 Yellow Onion, diced
- 1 tsp Garam Masala
- Kosher Salt, to taste
- 1 Lime, zested and juiced
- 4 cups of Vegetable Stock
- 1-inch knob Ginger
- 1 - 14 ounce can of Coconut Milk
- Olive Oil
- 4 Carrots, peeled and chopped
- 2 Bay Leaves
- 2 Jalapeño, diced
- 1/2 tsp Cumin
- 1/2 tsp Coriander
- 3 Garlic Cloves, chopped
- 2 Roma Tomatoes, chopped
- Cilantro, Lime Wedges, and Sour Cream for garnish

Instructions

1. Put a few tbsp of olive oil in a large pot and set it over medium-low heat.
2. Put in the tomato, onion, and jalapeño. Sauté for five minutes.
3. Throw in the bay leaves, spices, garlic, ginger, and carrots. Mix everything for a minute or two.
4. Put in the vegetable stock and lentils.
5. Cover and cook on lower heat for thirty minutes or until the lentils are very soft.
6. To make the soup smooth, use a KitchenAid immersion blender.
7. Then, add the lime juice and coconut milk and season with kosher salt to taste.
8. Add olive oil, sour cream, lime juice, and cilantro to serve.

15. CHILLED CREAMY PEA AND MINT SOUP

Prep Time: 20 Minutes | Cook Time: 15 Minutes

Total Time: 30 Minutes | Serving: 4

Ingredients

- 100ml dollop cream
- 60g baby spinach
- 1L chicken or vegetable stock
- 800g baby peas
- 1 tbsp extra virgin olive oil
- Salt a& pepper
- 1 clove garlic, chopped
- 1 onion, diced
- 1 bunch mint, leaves picked (reserving a few leaves for the garnish)

Instructions

1. Put a few tbsp of olive oil in a large pot and set it over medium-low heat.
2. Put in the tomato, onion, and jalapeño. Sauté for five minutes.
3. Throw in the bay leaves, spices, garlic, ginger, and carrots. Mix everything for a minute or two.
4. Put in the vegetable stock and lentils.
5. Cover and cook on lower heat for 30 minutes or until the lentils are very soft.
6. To make the soup smooth, use a KitchenAid immersion blender.
7. Then, add the lime juice and coconut milk and season with kosher salt to taste.
8. Add olive oil, sour cream, lime juice, and cilantro to serve.

16. THAI RED CURRY SOUP

Prep Time: 25 Minutes | Cook Time: 25 Minutes

Total Time: 50 Minutes | Serving: 6

Ingredients

- 2 tbsp olive oil, divided
- 1 medium onion, diced
- ¼ tsp ground black pepper
- ¼ cup of fresh cilantro leaves, chopped
- 1 large red bell pepper, diced
- ¼ tsp kosher salt
- ¼ cup of fresh basil leaves, chopped
- 18 large shrimp, peeled and deveined
- 1 tbsp grated fresh ginger

- 2 tsp brown sugar
- 2 tsp fish sauce
- 1 (8.8 ounces) pouch of rice Jasmine
- 4 cups of unsalted chicken stock
- 3 green onions, thinly sliced
- 1 tbsp fresh lime juice
- 3 tbsp red curry paste
- 3 cloves garlic, minced
- 1 (13.5 ounce) can light coconut milk

Instructions

1. In a big Dutch oven, heat 1 tbsp of olive oil over medium heat. Add salt and pepper to the shrimp. Turn the shrimp over halfway through cooking for two to three minutes or until it turns pink. Put away.
2. Put the bell pepper, onion, garlic, and olive oil into the pot. Stirring now and then, cook for about three minutes or until tender. Add ginger and curry paste and mix well for one minute or until it smells good.
3. Add the rice, stock, and coconut milk and stir them in. Scrape the bottom of the pot to get rid of any brown bits.
4. Bring to a boil over high heat. Lower the heat and cook, stirring now and then, for about 10 minutes until the liquid is almost gone. Add the sugar and fish sauce and mix well. Take it off the heat.
5. Puree the soup in the pot with a KitchenAid immersion blender.
6. Add the lime juice, cilantro, basil, and green onions and mix them in. Put equal amounts of soup into 6 bowls, and then add three shrimp to each one. Serve right away.

17. THAI COCONUT CURRY CARROT SOUP

Prep Time: 20 Minutes | Cook Time: 2 Hour 1 Minutes

Total Time: 2 Hour 21 Minutes | Serving: 1

Ingredients

- ¼ cup of Curry Paste
- 2 tbsp Avocado Oil
- 5 cups of Carrots, Chopped
- 1 tsp Ground Ginger
- 1 tbsp Curry Spice
- 1 cup of Vegetable Stock
- 2 Cans full-fat coconut milk
- 2 tbsp Coconut Aminos (or Soy Sauce)
- 1 Yellow Onion, Chopped
- ½ tbsp Garlic, Minced
- Salt to taste, Chili flakes for garnish
- Optional: Naan, Sourdough, or gluten-free bread for dipping

Instructions

1. In a big pot, heat 2 tbsp of avocado oil.
2. Put chopped onion and minced garlic into the pot. Cook on low for two to three minutes, until the onion is transparent and smells good.
3. Put in the pot cans of coconut milk (with the cream on top) and vegetable stock. Mix well until there are no more chunks. Stir again after adding the curry paste and coconut aminos.
4. Spices like curry, ginger, and salt should be added to taste. Stir.
5. Add the chopped carrots and mix them in. Turn the heat down to low, cover, and cook for 2 hours until the carrots are soft.
6. Puree the soup with a KitchenAid immersion blender until it is smooth and creamy. If you like, you can also leave it chunkier. You can also put it in a blender and blend it that way.
7. Add chili flakes and serve with fresh naan, sourdough, or gluten-free bread. Enjoy!

18. THAI COCONUT CURRY SOUP

Prep Time: 10 Minutes | Cook Time: 20 Minutes

Total Time: 30 Minutes | Serving: 4

Ingredients

- 5 cloves garlic, chopped
- 2 tbsp olive oil
- 1" ginger, chopped
- 1 tsp salt
- 2 cup of vegetable broth
- 2 14-ounce cans of coconut milk
- 1 tbsp turmeric
- 2 tbsp red curry paste
- 1/2 onion, roughly chopped
- 4 carrots, cubed
- 2 tbsp coconut sugar
- 1 large sweet potato, cubed
- optional toppings: tofu, cabbage, mushroom, lime, cilantro, mint, lime

Instructions

1. In a Dutch oven, warm olive oil over medium-low heat.
2. Spice up the pot by adding the garlic, ginger, and onion. For about 4 minutes, cook until the onion is soft, smells good, and starts to turn brown.
3. Mix in the red curry paste and the spices. Keep cooking for two more minutes.
4. Add the carrots, coconut milk, vegetable broth, and sweet potatoes now. Add some water and stir it around. About 15 minutes of cooking time is enough to make the carrots and sweet potatoes soft. Make sure to scrape and stir the pan's bottom.
5. Let the soup cool down before putting it in the KitchenAid immersion blender. Make the soup smooth and creamy by blending it.
6. Serve with extra vegetables or tofu.

19. THAI CURRY CARROT SOUP

Prep Time: 20 Minutes | Cook Time: 15 Minutes

Total Time: 35 Minutes | Serving: 4

Ingredients

- Cilantro and Sesame Seeds to top
- 2 cups of Broth vegetable or chicken
- 1 Lime juiced
- 2 cloves garlic minced
- 1 tbsp Ghee or Coconut Oil or Olive Oil
- 1 13.5-ounce can of Coconut Milk
- 1.5 inches ginger peeled and minced
- 1 Onion yellow or red
- 2 tbsp Thai Red Curry Paste
- Salt and pepper to taste
- 5 cups of Carrots, just about 2 pounds

Instructions

1. Turn on the Instant Pot to "Sauté" and chop the onion.
2. Put in the oil and heat it.
3. And then add the chopped onions. Cook for five minutes or until the onions are soft and transparent.
4. Place the Thai Red Curry Paste, ginger, and garlic in the pan. Cook for a few minutes.
5. Remove the "Sauté" setting and add the broth, lime juice, and carrots.
6. Put the food in the Instant Pot and set it to high pressure.
7. When it's done cooking, turn the valve to the vent to let out the pressure that has built up. Then, wait for it to cool down completely before opening the lid.
8. Put the coconut milk and blend the soup with the KitchenAid immersion blender to make the soup smooth.
9. Add salt and pepper, then sprinkle cilantro and sesame seeds on top.
10. Serve and have fun!

20. CURRIED BUTTERNUT SQUASH SOUP

Prep Time: 5 Minutes | Cook Time: 25 Minutes

Total Time: 30 Minutes | Serving: 4

Ingredients

Soup:

- 2 medium shallots (thinly diced)
- 1-3 tbsp maple syrup (or sub coconut sugar)
- 1 pinch each sea salt + black pepper (plus more to taste)
- 1 14-ounce can of light coconut milk
- 1 1/2 tbsp curry powder
- 1 tbsp coconut or avocado oil

- 1/4 tsp ground cinnamon
- 2 cups of vegetable broth
- 6 cups of peeled & chopped butternut squash
- 2 cloves garlic, minced (2 cloves yield 1 tbsp or 6 g)
- 1-2 tsp chili garlic paste (optional)

For Serving Optional:

- Full-fat coconut milk
- Toasted pumpkin seeds

- Chili garlic paste

Instructions

1. Warm up a big pot on medium to low heat.
2. Put in the garlic, shallots, and oil once it's hot. Stirring often, cook for two minutes.
3. Salt, pepper, curry powder, and ground cinnamon should all be added along with the butternut squash. Mix to cover. Then, put the lid on and cook for 4 minutes, stirring now and then.
4. Add chili garlic paste, maple syrup or coconut sugar, vegetable broth, and coconut milk for extra heat.
5. Over medium-low heat, bring to a low boil. Reduce the heat, cover, and simmer for 15 minutes or until the butternut squash is soft enough to pierce with a fork.
6. Purée on high with a KitchenAid immersion blender until smooth and creamy. If you used a blender, put the soup back in the pot.
7. If you need to, add more curry powder, salt, or sweetener based on your taste. Over medium-low heat, keep cooking for a few more minutes.
8. You can serve it plain or with any toppings you like. Covered leftovers can be kept in the refrigerator for three to four days or in the freezer for up to one month. Fresh is best.

21. THAI SWEET POTATO SOUP

Prep Time: 20 Minutes | Cook Time: 40 Minutes

Total Time: 1 Hour | Serving: 4

Ingredients

- 3 tbsp. red curry paste
- 1 tbsp olive oil
- 4 medium sweet potatoes, peeled and chopped
- 4 cups of vegetable stock
- 3 cloves garlic, peeled and minced
- 1 14-ounce can full-fat coconut milk
- 3 tbsp. lime juice
- 1 yellow onion, chopped
- 1 tbsp fresh ginger, minced (or 1 tbsp. ground ginger)
- 1 tsp salt + more to taste

Instructions

1. Set a big pot or Dutch oven on medium heat. Put in the garlic, onion, and olive oil. Cook for about two minutes, until the onion is soft. After you add the curry paste, cook for two more minutes.
2. Put in the ginger, sweet potatoes, and vegetable stock. Let it cook on low heat for 15 minutes or until the potatoes are soft. Mix well after adding salt, lime juice, and coconut milk. Mix all the ingredients using a KitchenAid immersion blender. Takes about 3 to 4 minutes to blend until smooth.
3. Add some coconut milk or fresh herbs on top. Warm up and serve.

22. CHICKEN BUTTERNUT SQUASH SOUP

Prep Time: 20 Minutes | Cook Time: 1 Hour

Total Time: 1 Hour 20 Minutes | Serving: 8

Ingredients

- ½ tsp Thyme
- 1 tsp Salt
- 5 Cups of Butternut Squash cut into cubes
- 2 cans Cannellini Beans 15-ounce cans, drained
- 4 Cups of Gluten Free Chicken Broth
- 1 Cup of Yellow Onion diced (about 1 medium onion)
- ½ tsp Red Pepper Flakes
- ½ tsp Black Pepper
- ½ Cup of Non-Dairy Cream
- ½ Cup of Celery diced (1-2 stalks)
- 4 slices Thick Cut Bacon cut into ½" pieces
- 4 Cups of Cooked Chicken
- 3 Cups of spinach roughly chopped
- 3 cloves garlic minced

Instructions

1. In a big Dutch oven, cook the bacon over medium heat.
2. When crisp, remove the bacon to a plate lined with paper kitchen towels. Take out the fat, but save 2 tablespoons.
3. Put the celery and onions in the pot. Stirring now and then, cook for about 5 minutes or until softened.
4. Salt, red pepper, thyme, and black pepper should be added. Stir the food all the time for one minute.
5. After adding the squash, pour the chicken broth into the pot. Bring to a low boil. Reduce the heat, cover, and cook for 15 to 20 minutes or until the squash is soft enough to pierce with a fork.
6. Begin to cook the soup. Open a can of beans and put half of them in a bowl. Add about a cup of cooked squash to the same bowl when it's done. You can blend with a fork or a KitchenAid immersion blender.
7. Take off the lid. Put in the chicken, bacon pieces, and the rest of the beans. Add the bean puree and mix it in. Bring the heat back down to low and cook for another 5 minutes.
8. After you add the spinach, cook for three more minutes.
9. Take it off the heat. Add the cream and mix it in well.
10. Add more bacon pieces and roasted pepitas as a garnish and serve right away.

23. SPICY CREAMY CHICKEN POBLANO SOUP

Prep Time: 20 Minutes | Cook Time: 1 Hour

Total Time: 1 Hour 20 Minutes | Serving: 8

Ingredients

- 3 garlic cloves minced
- 1 tsp freshly ground black pepper
- 3 medium poblano peppers seeded and diced
- 6 cups of chicken broth
- 1 ½ tsp kosher salt
- 2 cups of heavy cream
- 1 tsp ground cumin
- 4 raw boneless skinless chicken breasts

- 2 large carrots peeled and diced
- ¼ cup of chopped fresh cilantro
- 1 tsp dried thyme
- 1 large white onion
- 3 celery stalks diced
- 8 tbsp unsalted butter
- tortilla chips and sliced radishes for garnish

Instructions

1. In a large pot, melt the butter over medium-high heat. It will take about 15 minutes to cook after adding the chopped onions, celery, carrots, garlic, and poblanos. Put in the thyme, cumin, salt, and pepper. Add 5 more minutes of cooking.
2. It will boil when you add the broth, then turn the heat down to medium-low and add the raw chicken. Put the lid on top and cook for fifteen minutes or until the chicken is fully cooked.
3. Put the cooked chicken on a plate and shred it. Put away.
4. Pour heavy cream into the soup pot and mix it well.
5. Blend the soup slowly with a KitchenAid immersion blender until it is smooth.
6. Put the chicken shreds back into the pot. Add the cilantro. Add 10 more minutes of simmering time to bring the flavors together.
7. Rash slices, tortilla strips, and cilantro should be served on the side.

24. CREAMY CAULIFLOWER SOUP

Prep Time: 20 Minutes | Cook Time: 6 Hour

Total Time: 6 Hour 20 Minutes | Serving: 14

Ingredients

- 6 cups of water
- 1-1/2 tsp salt
- 1 large bay leaf
- 1-1/2 tsp adobo seasoning
- 3 garlic cloves, minced
- 1 small onion, chopped
- 3 tsp dried celery flakes
- 3/4 cup of nonfat dry milk powder
- 3/4 tsp ground mustard
- 1 medium head cauliflower (about 1-1/2 pounds)
- 1/4 tsp cayenne pepper
- 1-3/4 pounds Yukon Gold potatoes, peeled and cut into 1-inch cubes
- Optional toppings: Shredded cheddar cheese, sliced green onions and croutons

Instructions

1. Place the first 10 items in a 6-quart slow cooker. Sprinkle milk powder on top after adding water.
2. Cover and cook on low for six to eight hours or until the cauliflower is very soft. Take out the bay leaf. Use a KitchenAid immersion blender to blend the soup. Then, put it back in the slow cooker and heat it through. Serve with toppings if you want.

25. PARSNIP & CELERY ROOT BISQUE

Prep Time: 25 Minutes | Cook Time: 45 Minutes . Total Time: 1 Hour 10 Minutes | Serving: 8

Ingredients

- 1-1/2 tsp salt
- 6 cups of chicken stock
- 1-1/2 pounds parsnips, peeled and chopped (about 4 cups)
- 3/4 tsp coarsely ground pepper
- 2 tbsp minced fresh chives
- 1 cup of heavy whipping cream
- 2 tbsp olive oil
- 2 tsp lemon juice
- 1 medium celery root, peeled and cubed (about 1-1/2 cups)
- 4 garlic cloves, minced
- 2 medium leeks (white portion only), chopped (about 2 cups)
- 2 tbsp minced fresh parsley
- Pomegranate seeds, optional

Instructions

1. Put oil in a large saucepan and heat it over medium-high heat. Sauté the leeks for three minutes. Put in the celery root and parsnips. Cook and stir for 4 minutes. Bring it to a boil and stir in the garlic. Mix in the salt, pepper, and stock. Bring everything together to a boil. Turn down the heat and cover the pot. Let the vegetables cook for 25 to 30 minutes.
2. Use a KitchenAid immersion blender to blend the soup. Put the blended soup back into the pot. Mix in the lemon juice, cream, and parsley. Heat everything through. If you want, you can serve it with chives and pomegranate seeds.

26. CREAMY BUTTERNUT SQUASH & SAGE SOUP

Prep Time: 20 Minutes | Cook Time: 50 Minutes

Total Time: 1 Hour 10 Minutes | Serving: 4

Ingredients

- 2 tbsp minced fresh sage
- 1/4 tsp pepper
- 4 cups of cubed peeled butternut squash
- 1 tbsp olive oil
- 1/4 tsp salt

Soup:

- 1/8 tsp pepper
- 1 garlic clove, minced
- 3/4 tsp salt
- 4 cups of water
- 2 tbsp butter, divided
- 1/4 to 1/2 tsp crushed red pepper flakes
- 1 medium onion, chopped
- 1 medium sweet potato, chopped
- 1 tbsp olive oil
- 1 medium carrot, chopped

Instructions

1. Warm the oven up to 400°. Put the squash in a 15x10x1-inch baking pan lined with foil. Put some oil on top and add sage, salt, and pepper. Toss to cover. Stirring occasionally, roast for 30 to 35 minutes or until tender.
2. At the same time, heat oil and 1 tbsp butter in a big saucepan over medium heat. Stir the onion and garlic in for three to four minutes or until they soften. Lower the heat to medium to low, and cook, stirring now and then, for 30 to 40 minutes or until the food is a deep golden brown. Add pepper, salt, and pepper flakes and mix well.
3. Put carrot, sweet potato, and water in a saucepan. Bring up the temperature. Lower the heat and cook the uncovered vegetables for 10 to 15 minutes or until soft. Add the squash mixture and the rest of the butter to the soup. Use a KitchenAid immersion blender to blend the soup. Put the blended soup back in the pan and heat it through.

27. CREAMY ROOT VEGGIE SOUP

Prep Time: 15 Minutes | Cook Time: 1 Hour

Total Time: 1 Hour 15 Minutes | Serving: 8

Ingredients

- 4 bacon strips, chopped
- 2 tsp minced fresh thyme
- 1 bay leaf
- 3 garlic cloves, minced
- 6 medium parsnips, peeled and cubed (about 4 cups)
- Additional minced fresh thyme
- 1 tsp salt
- 1 cup of heavy whipping cream
- 1 large celery root, peeled and cubed (about 5 cups)
- 1 large onion, chopped
- 1/4 tsp ground nutmeg
- 6 cups of chicken stock
- 1/4 tsp white pepper

Instructions

1. In a Dutch oven, cook the bacon over medium-low heat, stirring occasionally, until crispy. Drain on paper towels after taking them out with a slotted spoon. In the bacon grease, stir the onion for 6 to 8 minutes or until soft. Cook for one more minute after adding the garlic.
2. Include celery root, parsnips, stock, and a bay leaf. Get it boiling. Lower the heat and cook the uncovered vegetables for 30 to 40 minutes or until soft. Ignore the bay leaf.
3. To puree soup, use a KitchenAid immersion blender. Allow to cool a bit, then blend in batches in a blender and add to the pan. Add cream, salt, pepper, nutmeg, and 2 tsp of thyme. Stir well and heat through. Add more bacon and thyme to each serving.

28. CREAMY MISO VEGGIE SOUP

Prep Time: 5 Minutes | Cook Time: 15 Minutes

Total Time: 20 Minutes | Serving: 4

Ingredients

- 3 tbsp white miso paste
- 3 cups of vegetable broth
- ¼ cup of butter or vegan butter
- 3 cloves garlic, minced
- 2 cups of leftover vegetables, diced
- 1 tsp salt
- ¼ tsp cayenne pepper

Instructions

1. Put the butter in a pan and melt it over medium heat.
2. Add miso and stir until it is fully mixed in with the butter.
3. Add the chopped garlic, salt, cayenne pepper, and any vegetables that are still left over. Cook the vegetables for eight to ten minutes until they get soft.
4. Increase the heat and add the vegetable broth. Put the mixture into a KitchenAid immersion blender and mix it until it is creamy and smooth. Enjoy.

29. CREAMY ZUCCHINI SOUP WITH WALNUTS AND DILL

Prep Time: 10 Minutes | Cook Time: 10 Minutes

Total Time: 20 Minutes | Serving: 6

Ingredients

- 1 medium yellow onion, chopped
- 2 garlic cloves, cut into quarters
- 4 medium zucchini, halved lengthwise and thinly sliced
- 4 cups of chicken broth (such as Swanson Organic)
- 1 tsp salt
- ¼ tsp freshly ground black pepper
- ½ cup of walnuts toasted
- 3 tbsp freshly squeezed lemon juice from 1 lemon
- 3 tbsp extra virgin olive oil, divided, plus more for drizzling
- 2 tbsp fresh dill or 1 tbsp dried, plus more for serving

Instructions

1. Warm the oven up to 350° F. Line a baking sheet with aluminum foil or parchment paper for easy cleanup.
2. In a large pot, heat two tbsp of the oil over medium-low heat. After you add the onion and garlic, stir them around a lot for about five minutes or until the onions are soft and transparent. Don't turn brown.
3. Turn on the heat and add the chicken broth, salt, and pepper. Low-level the heat, cover, and let it cook for 10 to 12 minutes until the zucchini is soft.
4. Put the walnuts on the baking sheet that has been prepared and toast them in the oven for 5 to 10 minutes until they smell good.
5. Put the walnuts and dill into the soup. Blend the soup until it's smooth with a KitchenAid immersion blender. Make sure you don't fill the jar up. Leave the lid's hole open and cover it loosely with a dish towel to let the heat escape.
6. Add the lemon juice and the last tbsp of oil to the soup. Check the seasoning and add salt if needed (I usually add about ¼ tsp more). Put some soup in bowls, drizzle with olive oil, and top with dill.
7. You can freeze the soup for up to three months. It must be defrosted in the fridge for 12 hours to 1 day or until completely thawed. Enjoy.

30. BROCCOLI, ARUGULA, AND GOAT'S CHEESE SOUP

Prep Time: 5 Minutes | Cook Time: 15 Minutes

Total Time: 20 Minutes | Serving: 4

Ingredients

- 3 ounce goat's cheese
- 6 ounce broccoli, cut into floret-sized pieces
- 5 cups of water
- about 1 bag of greens, use a mix of arugula and spinach
- 1 onion, diced
- 1 tbsp olive oil
- 1 tbsp of bouillon base or a stock cube
- salt & pepper

Instructions

1. Put the soup pot on medium-high heat and add the olive oil. Let the onion cook for two to three minutes until it gets soft.
2. Bring the water, broccoli, and bouillon base to a simmer.
3. Wait about 10 minutes until the broccoli is soft. The greens should be added and wilted.
4. Use a KitchenAid immersion blender to make the soup smooth.
5. Spice it up with salt and pepper and goat cheese. Add more of the blend.
6. Adjust the seasonings based on your taste.
7. Include avocado toast to get even more of the healthy greens.

31. CHICKEN CORN CHOWDER

Prep Time: 20 Minutes | Cook Time: 40 Minutes

Total Time: 1 Hour 10 Minutes | Serving: 6

Ingredients

- 1/2 tsp paprika
- 1 tsp salt
- 2 tbsp salted butter
- 1 red bell pepper, diced
- 1 tsp ground mustard
- 1 1/2 cups of whole milk
- 1 tsp garlic powder
- 1 pound baby yellow potatoes, diced
- 1 pound chicken breast
- 1 tbsp cornstarch + 2 tbsp water
- 2 15ounce cans of corn, drained
- 1 quart of chicken stock
- 1 jalapeno, diced
- 1/2 tsp pepper
- 1 tbsp minced garlic
- 1 small yellow onion, diced

Optional Toppings:

- Sliced green onion
- Bacon bits
- Shredded cheddar cheese

Instructions

1. Warm up a big pot over medium heat. Put in 2 tbsp of butter and melt it.
2. It takes about 5 minutes for the onions and peppers to get soft after you add the butter.
3. After that, add the garlic that has been chopped up and cook for one more minute.
4. Put in the spices and mix well. Add the corn, chicken stock, milk, and diced potatoes after it's been mixed. Make sure that the chicken is immersed in the water.
5. Bring to a boil, then put a lid on top. Turn the heat down to a low level and cook for 30 minutes or until the chicken is fully cooked.
6. Take the chicken out of the soup and shred it. Put it away until we blend the soup.
7. Add 2 tbsp of cold water to 1 tbsp of cornstarch and mix well. Mix it well into the soup after adding it. Bring it back up to speed and let it boil for one minute. This will help the soup get thicker.
8. Blend about half of the soup with a KitchenAid immersion blender. How thick you want the soup to be will determine how much you blend! To blend the soup without an immersion blender, you can take a cupful out of the pot and put it in a blender. Then, put the soup back into the pot.
9. Put the chicken back in and mix everything.
10. Add your favorite toppings right away and serve!

32. CHICKEN AND RICE SOUP

Prep Time: 5 Minutes | Cook Time: 25 Minutes

Total Time: 30 Minutes | Serving: 5

Ingredients

- ½ to ¾ tsp salt
- 1 cup of chopped onion
- 3 tbsp olive oil
- ¼ tsp cayenne powder or use less if you'd like
- 3 to 4 garlic cloves chopped
- 2 14.5-ounce cans of chicken stock
- 2 to 3 boneless skinless chicken thighs
- 2 tsp coriander powder
- ½ cup of rice rinsed and drained (basmati or jasmine)
- 2 carrots medium to large, peeled and chopped

Instructions

1. In a pot, heat the olive oil over medium-low heat. Add the chopped onion and garlic and cook for three to five minutes, until the onion turns transparent.
2. Add the coriander and cayenne powders and stir them in. Cook while stirring for about one minute or until the spices are golden.
3. Bring the stock, carrots, rice, chicken thighs, and salt to a boil. Then, cover it with a lid, lower the warmth, and cook until the rice is soft and the chicken is cooked all through.
4. Take the chicken thighs off the heat and put them on a plate. Let them cool down while you blend the soup.
5. Blend the soup with a KitchenAid immersion blender until it is thick and creamy.
6. Let's shred the chicken. Using two big forks, break the chicken thighs into big chunks and add them to the already blended soup. If the soup seems too thick, add more stock and mix it in.
7. Put it in bowls and serve it with chopped cilantro on top.

33. LOW CARB SPICY CHICKEN ENCHILADA SOUP

Prep Time: 10 Minutes | Cook Time: 30 Minutes

Total Time: 40 Minutes | Serving: 6

Ingredients

- 1 tsp fresh cilantro
- 1 tsp mesquite liquid smoke
- 1 tsp garlic
- 3 cups of cooked boneless, skinless chicken breasts
- 10 ounces Rotel tomatoes & chilies
- 1/2 cup of raw red bell pepper
- 1-quart low-sodium, low-fat chicken broth

- 2 tbsp canned diced green chiles
- 2 cups of water
- 2 tbsp ground cumin
- Monterey Jack and cheddar cheese blend
- 1 tbsp ground ancho chili pepper
- Sour cream (optiona)

Instructions

1. Warm up the covered pot.
2. Spray nonstick cooking spray on a pot and add 1/2 cup of diced red bell pepper.
3. Put in chicken stock.
4. Season the broth with chili, cumin, garlic, liquid smoke, and cilantro.
5. Turn on the heat and add the chicken to the broth.
6. Put 2 cups of water and a can of diced tomatoes with chilies (and juice) in a bowl. Use a KitchenAid immersion blender to blend it into a puree. After that, put it in the soup pot.
7. Let it cook for 20 minutes so the flavors can blend.
8. Put it in bowls of hot soup.
9. Add cheddar or jack cheese on top.
10. You can add sour cream on top if you'd like.
11. If needing a low-carb crunch, consider a few pork rinds.

34. CHICKEN TORTILLA SOUP

Prep Time: 10 Minutes | Cook Time: 25 Minutes

Total Time: 35 Minutes | Serving: 12

Ingredients

- 2 tbsp Roasted Garlic, mashed OR
- 2 tbsp Fresh Garlic, minced
- 1 tsp Kosher Salt
- 5 cups of Broth Vegetable or Chicken
- 1/4 tsp Cayenne Pepper
- 2 tsp Olive Oil
- 1 tsp Ground Cumin
- 1 tsp Ground Coriander
- 1/2 tsp Dried Oregano
- 1 1/2 cups of onion, diced

- 2 1/2 cups of Frozen Corn (divided)
- 2 cups of Cooked Chicken, shredded or diced (can be baked, grilled or roasted)
- 1 tbsp Fresh Lime Juice
- 5 Corn Tortillas, cut into wedges (6-inch tortillas)
- 2 –15 ounce cans of roasted Tomatoes, diced

Instructions

1. Heat 2 tsp of olive oil over medium heat in a large stock pot.
2. After adding the onions, cook them for 5 to 6 minutes until they become soft and golden.
3. If you're using raw garlic, mix it with the tortilla wedges and cook for another 4 to 5 minutes, until the tortillas get soft and the garlic turns clear. (Add roasted garlic with the corn and tomatoes so the garlic doesn't stick to the bottom of the pan.)
4. For every 192 grams of frozen corn kernels, add 1 1/2 cups of broth and spices. Use a stir to mix. If you have roasted garlic, add it to the pot with the tomatoes and corn.
5. Bring the mix to a boil, turn down the heat, and let it cook for 5 minutes.
6. Use a KitchenAid immersion blender to blend all the soup ingredients until the soup is creamy and smooth. Add the blended soup back to the pot.
7. Back up the soup to a boil over medium-low heat, then turn it down to a simmer.
8. Add the extra 81 grams (cup) of corn, lime juice, and chicken.
9. Keep cooking on low heat for another 10 minutes.
10. Take it off the heat and serve.
11. If you want, you can add avocado or sour cream and tortilla strips as a garnish.

35. CHICKEN CORDON BLEU SOUP

Prep Time: 15 Minutes | Cook Time: 25 Minutes

Total Time: 40 Minutes | Serving: 6

Ingredients

- 2 cups of half-and-half cream
- 1 medium onion, chopped
- 2 cups of chicken broth
- 1 tbsp Dijon mustard
- 1 tsp salt
- 1 garlic clove, minced
- 1 small head cauliflower, coarsely chopped

- 2 cups of shredded Swiss cheese
- 2 tbsp butter
- 2 tbsp olive oil
- 3 tbsp all-purpose flour
- 1/2 tsp pepper
- 1 cup of finely cubed fully cooked ham
- 2 cups of shredded cooked chicken

Instructions

1. Put butter and oil in a large saucepan and heat them over medium-high heat. It will take eight to ten minutes to cook and stir after you add the cauliflower and onion. Put the garlic in the pot and cook for one minute until it smells good. After that, add the flour and mix it well. Then, add the broth slowly while whisking. Bring to a boil while stirring all the time. Continue to stir and cook for 12 to 15 minutes or until the cauliflower is soft.

2. Use a KitchenAid immersion blender to blend the soup. Or, let the soup cool a bit and mix it in batches in a blender. Put the blended soup back into the pan. Put in the ham, mustard, chicken, cream, salt, and pepper. Heat everything through. Add cheese and stir until it melts.

36. MILDLY THICK HEARTY BEEF BARLEY SOUP

Prep Time: 10 Minutes | Cook Time: 20 Minutes

Total Time: 30 Minutes | Serving: 4

Ingredients

- 2 bay leaves
- Salt & pepper
- 8 cup of beef broth
- 2 medium carrots chopped
- 2 cloves garlic, minced
- 2 celery stalks chopped
- 2 cups of leftover beef roast cubed
- ½ cup of uncooked barley
- ½ large onion chopped
- 1 14-ounce can of whole tomatoes

Instructions

1. Boil the barley. Put away.
2. Put the onion, celery, and carrots in a large soup pot and heat it over medium-low heat. After 5 minutes, the food should be soft. Add pepper and salt.
3. After you add the garlic, cook for another 30 seconds.
4. Put in the tomato sauce and beef broth. Use a spoon to crush the tomatoes so their juices come out.
5. Bring to a boil after adding the bay leaves. Turn down the heat and let it cook slowly for 10 minutes.
6. Put the beef roast cubes into the soup broth and let them heat up.
7. Take out the bay leaves and add the cooked barley right at the end.
8. Use a KitchenAid immersion blender to blend. Mix until it's smooth.
9. Enjoy while still warm!

37. VELVETY VEGETABLE-TURKEY SOUP

Prep Time: 15 Minutes | Cook Time: 1 Hour 45 Minutes

Total Time: 2 Hours | Serving: 12

Ingredients

- 1 large onion
- 1 pound turkey or chicken necks
- 1 small carrot
- 1 large parsnip
- 1/2 pound turkey roll, finely diced
- Black pepper, to taste
- 2 tsp salt
- 10 cups of water
- 2 large potatoes
- 3 small zucchini, peeled

Instructions

1. Put the turkey necks and water into a large pot. Bring up the temperature.
2. As the water heats up, cut the vegetables into big pieces and add them to the pot with salt and pepper. After boiling the water, turn down the heat and let it cook for another hour and a half.
3. Take the necks out of the soup. You can take pieces of turkey meat from the necks and add them to the soup if you want to. Then, you can throw away the bones. Blend the soup until it's smooth with a KitchenAid immersion blender.
4. Bring it back to a boil after adding the turkey roll dice. Turn off the heat and taste the food to see if it needs more seasoning.

38. CHICKEN POTATO SOUP

Prep Time: 15 Minutes | Cook Time: 45 Minutes

Total Time: 1 Hour | Serving: 6

Ingredients

- 1/8 tsp cayenne pepper
- 1/4 tsp salt
- 1/4 tsp black pepper
- 2 1/2 cups of water
- 1/2 cup of onion finely chopped
- 6 cups of potatoes
- 1/2 cup of Greek yogurt low-fat
- 1/2 cup of 2% milk
- 3 cups of broth chicken
- 1 cup of chicken shredded
- 2 tsp olive oil extra virgin
- 1/3 cup of carrot grated

Instructions

1. Cut the onion up very small. Grate the carrot. Leave the carrot alone.
2. Warm up some olive oil in a big stock pot. Put in the chopped onion and cook for three to five minutes.
3. Cut up potatoes after peeling them.
4. Put chopped potatoes, water, broth, salt, pepper, and cayenne pepper in a stock pot. Bring to a boil, lower the heat, and cook for 30 minutes until the potatoes are soft.
5. Take the pan off the heat when the potatoes are soft, and let the soup stop boiling and cool down. Put the KitchenAid immersion blender's chopping end under the liquid. Pulse the food slowly to break up some of the potatoes. Moving the blender around will help you blend the potatoes in three or four places. About half of the potato chunks should stay whole. Keep in mind that the soup is hot, so be careful.
6. Add chicken, milk, and grated carrots to the soup. Bring the soup back to a boil over medium-low heat.
7. Put a tbsp of Greek yogurt on top and serve.

39. ROASTED CAULIFLOWER SOUP

Prep Time: 20 Minutes | Cook Time: 1

Total Time: 1 Hour 20 Minutes | Serving: 6

Ingredients

- 1 tsp dried thyme
- 2 cups of heavy cream
- 2 heads cauliflower, separated into florets
- 2 shallots, chopped
- salt and pepper to taste
- 1 cup of water
- 3 cloves garlic, chopped
- 1 tbsp olive oil
- 3 cups of chicken broth
- 1 bay leaf

Instructions

1. Warm the oven up to 425° F (220 degrees C). Add the cauliflower pieces to a large bowl. Add the olive oil, garlic, and shallots. Spread out on a roasting pan with sides.
2. It will take about 30 minutes of roasting in a hot oven until it is toasted and soft.
3. Move the cauliflower to a soup pot when it's done, and add the chicken broth and water. Add the bay leaf and thyme, and then bring the dish to a boil. Put it on medium heat and cook for 30 minutes. Take the bay leaf off and throw it away.
4. Use a KitchenAid immersion blender to blend the soup in the pot. Do this in batches, then add the pureed batches back to the pot. Add the cream and season with salt and pepper. Warm everything up before you serve it, but don't boil it.

40. ROASTED RED PEPPER SOUP

Prep Time: 10 Minutes | Cook Time: 23 Minutes

Total Time: 33 Minutes | Serving: 8

Ingredients

- 4 large red bell peppers
- 4 Roma tomatoes cut in half
- 6 cloves garlic peeled
- 2 tbsp olive oil
- 1 medium onion diced
- 1 carrot diced
- 8 cups of chicken broth or vegetable broth
- 1 tsp Italian seasoning
- ¼ tsp red pepper flakes
- 1 tsp salt
- ½ cup of white wine, optional
- ½ cup of sour cream for serving, optional

Instructions

1. Warm the oven up to 425°F.
2. Cut each red pepper in half and take out the seeds and stems.
3. Put the tomatoes and bell peppers on a big baking sheet with the cut sides facing down.
4. Put the garlic cloves between the peppers and tomatoes if there is room.
5. Put the baking sheet in a hot oven and roast for 20 minutes.
6. To get some char on the vegetables' skin, put them under the broiler for three more minutes.
7. Set the oil in a big pot on the stove and heat it over medium to low heat.
8. Cook the carrot and onion until they become a little soft.
9. After you add the white wine, let it cook for 5 minutes.
10. It's time to add the salt, Italian seasoning, red pepper flakes, and broth.
11. Simmer on low heat and stir until the peppers and tomatoes are done.
12. Fire up the peppers, tomatoes, and garlic, then add them to the pot on the stove.
13. Puree the soup until it's smooth with a KitchenAid immersion blender.
14. Add some sour cream on top, and you can decorate with fresh basil.

41. ROASTED ROOT VEGETABLE SOUP

Prep Time: 15 Minutes | Cook Time: 1 Hour 15 Minutes

Total Time: 1 Hour 30 Minutes | Serving: 8

Ingredients

- 2 bunches (about 8 oz) Radishes, halved
- 1 pound Sweet Potatoes, diced
- 1/2 tsp Black Pepper
- 12 ounce Carrots, peeled and diced
- 2 tsp Fresh Thyme Leaves
- 2 tbsp Olive Oil
- 1 Red Onion, peeled and quartered
- 6 cloves Garlic, peeled
- 12 ounce Turnips, peeled and diced

For the Soup:

- 2 cups of Water
- 4 cups of Low Sodium Chicken Broth
- 4 ounce Parmesan or Pecorino Romano, grated
- 2-3 tsp Kosher Salt, to taste

Instructions

1. Put the radishes, carrots, sweet potatoes, and turnips in a bowl. Add the olive oil and black pepper. Put it on a half-sheet pan and bake it for 30 minutes at 425ºF.
2. Put the thyme, garlic, and red onion on the baking sheet and mix them all together. For another 20 to 25 minutes, until the vegetables are soft and the edges are turning brown, bake the dish.
3. With a KitchenAid immersion blender, blend the vegetables and chicken broth in a soup pot over medium-low heat until the soup is smooth.
4. Bring everything to a boil after adding the water. Then turn down the heat and let it cook slowly for 5 to 10 minutes. Set the cheese aside and add salt and pepper to taste.

42. ROASTED CAULIFLOWER & RED PEPPER SOUP

Prep Time: 50 Minutes | Cook Time: 25 Minutes

Total Time: 1 Hour 15 Minutes | Serving: 6

Ingredients

- 2 medium sweet red peppers, halved and seeded
- 1 large head cauliflower, broken into florets (about 7 cups)
- 4 tbsp olive oil, divided
- 1 cup of chopped sweet onion
- 2 garlic cloves, minced
- 2-1/2 tsp minced fresh rosemary or 3/4 tsp dried rosemary, crushed
- 1/2 tsp paprika
- 1/4 cup of all-purpose flour
- 4 cups of chicken stock
- 1 cup of 2% milk
- 1/2 tsp salt
- 1/4 tsp pepper
- 1/8 to 1/4 tsp cayenne pepper
- Shredded Parmesan cheese, optional

Instructions

1. Warm up the broiler. Put the peppers on a baking sheet lined with foil, skin side up. It will take about 5 minutes of broiling 4 inches away from the heat until the skins are blistered. Move to a bowl and cover. Let it sit for 20 minutes. Set the oven to bake and heat it to 400°.
2. Mix cauliflower with 2 tbsp of oil and spread it in a 15x10x1-inch pan. For twenty-five to thirty minutes, stirring now and then, roast until soft. Take the skin and seeds off of the peppers and chop them up.
3. Heat the last two tbsp of oil over medium-low heat in a 6-quart stockpot. Add the onion and cook, stirring now and then, for 6 to 8 minutes, until it turns golden and soft. Put in the paprika, rosemary, and garlic. Cook and stir for one minute. Add the flour and mix it in. Cook and stir for one minute. Slowly stir in the stock. While stirring all the time, bring to a boil. Cook and stir until it gets thick.
4. Add peppers and cauliflower and mix well. Use a KitchenAid immersion blender to blend the soup. Add the blended soup back to the pot. Add milk and the rest of the seasonings, then heat everything through. Serve with Parmesan if you want.

43. ROASTED BUTTERNUT SQUASH BISQUE WITH CINNAMON CASHEW CREAM

Prep Time: 10 Minutes | Cook Time: 1 Hour 15 Minutes

Total Time: 1 Hour 25 Minutes | Serving: 6

Ingredients

- 2 tbsp fresh ginger, minced
- 4 cups of vegetable broth
- 4 garlic cloves, minced
- ½ tsp salt, or to taste
- 1 tsp white wine vinegar, or to taste
- 1 tbsp olive oil
- 1 large butternut squash, halved and quartered
- 1 ½ tbsp olive oil
- 1 (13.66-ounce) can of coconut milk, lite or regular, both work
- 1 yellow onion, finely diced
- Some salt & black pepper
- Dash of ground cinnamon as garnish

For the Cinnamon Cashew Cream:

- 2 tsp lemon juice
- ½ cup of raw cashews (Fair Trade), soaked for 30 minutes
- ½ cup of water
- 1 tsp maple syrup
- ⅛ tsp salt
- 2 tbsp unsweetened coconut yogurt
- ¼ tsp ground cinnamon

Instructions

1. Warm the oven up to 375° F. Then, cut the butternut squash in half and scoop out the seeds and guts. Next, cut each half of the squash into four equal pieces. Sprinkle the squash pieces with salt and pepper, then rub them with olive oil and place them on a baking sheet skin side down. Once the oven is hot, bake the squash for about an hour or until a fork can quickly go through it.
2. Soak the ½ cup of raw cashews in hot water for 30 minutes while the squash is in the oven. The cashews should be soaked for 30 minutes. Then, drain them and blend them with ½ cup of water, salt, coconut yogurt, maple syrup, cinnamon, and lemon juice and until the mixture is smooth. Don't use the cashew cream until you're ready.
3. After taking the squash out of the oven to cool, heat 1 ½ tbsp of olive oil in a soup pot over medium heat. Add the onion, ginger, and garlic cloves and cook for seven to ten minutes until the onions become clearer and smell good. After that, put the vegetable broth in the soup pot and peel the butternut squash. Put the squash that has been peeled into the pot of soup.

4. Use a KitchenAid immersion blender to carefully blend the squash, onions, ginger, and garlic until the mixture is very creamy. A chunk or two of squash every once in a while is okay. Always keep the head of the immersion blender under the liquid so that the hot soup doesn't fly everywhere. Put the soup back on the heat and add the white wine vinegar, salt, and coconut cream. Blend until smooth. Mix those things well by stirring them.

5. After ensuring the soup is hot throughout, it's ready to be served. Add cinnamon cashew cream to a large bowl, then pour in some butternut squash bisque. Finally, sprinkle some ground cinnamon on top.

44. BROCCOLI AND CASHEW CREAM SOUP

Prep Time: 30 Minutes | Cook Time: 30 Minutes | Total Time: 1 Hour | Serving: 6

Ingredients

- 2 medium onions, diced
- 5 cloves garlic, minced
- 3 carrots, chopped
- 1/2 tsp red pepper
- 2 tsp extra-virgin olive oil
- 16 ounce broccoli (about 7 cups, packed)
- 2 stalks of celery, or one fennel bulb, chopped
- 1 1/2 tsp salt (to taste)
- 6 cups of water or vegetable stock dividend
- 1/2 cup of raw cashews, soaked

Instructions

1. In a small bowl, put the cashews. Put water on top (hot water makes the process go faster). Soak for around three hours or overnight.
2. Put oil in a big pot and set it on medium-high heat. Add the onion and a pinch of salt when the pan is hot. Sauté for three minutes.
3. Add the carrots and celery to finish cooking, and cook for five more minutes.
4. After you add the broccoli and garlic, cook for five more minutes.
5. Salt and pepper and five cups of water or vegetable stock should be added. Add water and stir. Bring to a boil. Once it starts to boil, reduce the heat and let it simmer for 15 minutes with the lid on.
6. Take out the cashews. Mix cashews with 1 cup of water or vegetable stock in a blender. Mix until it's very smooth and creamy. There shouldn't be any clumps. Leave the cashew cream alone.
7. To puree the soup, use a KitchenAid immersion blender. Most likely, you'll need to do this in groups.
8. Add the cashew cream after the soup has been pureed. Enjoy.

45. ROASTED ACORN SQUASH SOUP

Prep Time: 50 Minutes | Cook Time: 30 Minutes

Total Time: 1 Hour 20 Minutes | Serving: 4

Ingredients

- 1 tsp ground black pepper
- 1 shallot, chopped
- 2 carrots, chopped
- 1 granny smith apple, cored and chopped
- ¼ tsp dried sage
- ½ red onion, chopped
- ⅛ tsp cayenne pepper
- 1 tsp sea salt
- ½ yellow onion, chopped
- 3 acorn squashes
- 4 cups of vegetable stock
- ½ tsp dried ginger
- ⅛ tsp ground allspice
- 2 tbsp olive oil

Instructions

1. Warm the oven up to 400° F.
2. Line a baking sheet with foil or parchment paper.
3. Sprinkle some ground black pepper and kosher salt on top. Put the squash on the baking sheet and cut side down. Place in the oven and roast for 45 to 50 minutes or until the meat is soft and can be easily poked. Take it out of the oven and let it cool down.
4. When the meat is excellent, use a spoon to scoop out the meat from the skin. Throw away the skin and set the meat aside.
5. Warm up the olive oil in a big, deep pot over medium-high heat until it's hot. It will take about 6 to 8 minutes of cooking after adding the carrots, apple, shallot, and onions. Add the squash flesh, ginger, sage, cayenne, allspice, and vegetable stock when it's soft. Bring to a boil and stir well. Lower the heat and let it cook for 15 to 20 minutes.
6. Use a KitchenAid immersion blender to blend until the mixture is ready.
7. After the food has been pureed, add more salt or pepper to taste.

46. VEGAN CREAMY MUSHROOM SOUP

Prep Time: 20 Minutes | Cook Time: 25 Minutes

Total Time: 45 Minutes | Serving: 4

Ingredients

Cashew Cream:

- 1 3/4 cups of hot water
- 1 1/2 cups of raw cashews

Soup:

- 1/2 cup of No Cow Purely Plain Protein Powder
- 8 ounce mixed wild mushrooms, sliced thin
- 1/2 tsp salt
- 5 cloves garlic, minced
- 1 bay leaf
- 8 ounce cremini mushrooms, sliced thin
- 1 tbsp chopped fresh sage
- 1 large yellow onion, diced
- 1 tbsp balsamic vinegar
- 4 tbsp extra virgin olive oil, divided
- 1/4 tsp cracked black pepper
- 1 tbsp chopped fresh thyme
- 1 tbsp tamari or soy sauce
- 1/4 cup of dry white wine, optional 3-4 cups of vegetable stock

Serving:

- Chopped fresh parsley and thyme Toasted crusty bread.

Instructions

1. Put the cashews in a KitchenAid immersion blender at high speed and add the hot water on top of them. Allow the cashews to soak for 15 to 20 minutes.
2. Set a big pot over medium heat and add one tbsp of olive oil. Let the oil heat up while the cashews soak. Cook a quarter of the mushrooms (4 oz) until they turn brown, stirring occasionally. After that, take them out of the pot and set them aside until you're ready to serve the soup. Put the last three tbsp of olive oil in the same pot. Put in the garlic, tamari, bay leaf, thyme, sage, salt, pepper, and mushrooms. Also, add the onions. Stir the mushrooms occasionally for 10 to 12 minutes or until soft. Add the no-cow plain protein powder and stir it in. Cook for one more minute. Add dry white wine, and cook until most of the liquid is gone (about one to two minutes). Add 3 cups of vegetable broth, raise the heat to medium-high, and keep cooking until it starts to bubble. Simmer without cover for 10 minutes, stirring now and then.

3. Take the cashews out of the water and blend them with the water until they are very smooth. Pour into a bowl or measuring cup. Blend the cashews and add 1 1/2 cups of to the soup. Take the bay leaf out of the pot and throw it away. Use an immersion blender or put the soup in a blender and blend it until it's very smooth. Add the balsamic vinegar and the rest of the cashew cream to the pot, but save 1/4 cup of for garnish. Heat until the blending bubbles go away. If you think the soup is too thick, add up to a cup of more broth until it's the depth you like. Put the soup into bowls and top with the mushrooms you saved from step 2, the parsley, the thyme, and some cracked pepper. Pour the rest of the cashew cream on top and serve with crusty bread that has been toasted.

47. MUSHROOM & BROCCOLI SOUP

Prep Time: 20 Minutes | Cook Time: 45 Minutes

Total Time: 1 Hour 5 Minutes | Serving: 8

Ingredients

- 1 carton (32 ounces) vegetable broth
- 1/4 cup of finely chopped onion
- 2 celery ribs, finely chopped
- 1 tbsp canola oil
- 1 bunch broccoli (about 1-1/2 pounds)
- 1/2 pound sliced fresh mushrooms
- 2 tbsp lemon juice
- 2 cups of water
- 2 medium carrots, finely chopped
- 1 garlic clove, minced
- 1 tbsp reduced-sodium soy sauce

Instructions

1. Break up the broccoli florets into small pieces. Cut the stalks into small pieces.
2. Heat the oil in a big saucepan over medium-high heat. Add the mushrooms and cook for four to six minutes until soft. Add the soy sauce and stir it in. Take it out of the pan.
3. Put broccoli stalks, carrots, celery, onion, garlic, broth, and water in the same pan. Bring to a boil. Turn down the heat and let the vegetables simmer, uncovered, for twenty-five to thirty minutes until they are soft.
4. Use a KitchenAid immersion blender to blend the soup. Add mushrooms and florets and stir them in. Bring to a boil. Reduce the warm to medium and stir the broccoli for 8 to 10 minutes until it is soft. Add the lemon juice and stir.

48. CREAMY MUSHROOM CAULIFLOWER SOUP

Prep Time: 15 Minutes | Cook Time: 20 Minutes

Total Time: 35 Minutes | Serving: 4

Ingredients

- 1 can of coconut milk
- 1/2 tsp sea salt
- 3 garlic cloves, chopped
- 3 tbsp extra-virgin olive oil, divided
- 1 tsp fresh thyme leaves
- 5 ounce mixed mushrooms, chopped
- 1 head cauliflower, chopped (1/2 pound)
- 1/2 cup of onion, sliced
- 1/8 tsp white pepper
- 8 oz. cremini mushrooms, sliced
- 3 cups of water
- 2 packs Om Mighty Mushroom Broth
- 2 tbsp balsamic vinegar

Instructions

1. Over medium heat, cook the mushrooms and onion in a big pot with two tbsp of olive oil for about 5 minutes or until the onions become transparent.
2. Add the thyme and garlic and cook for 2 minutes, until the smell is pleasant.
3. Whisk in the Om Mighty Mushroom Broth and coconut milk until everything is well mixed.
4. Put water, balsamic vinegar, salt, and pepper in the cauliflower. Simmer for 10 to 14 minutes or until the cauliflower is very soft.
5. Use a KitchenAid immersion blender to blend until smooth. Put the lid back on the pot.
6. On medium heat, add the last tbsp of olive oil to a pan and add the mixed mushrooms. Cook for two to four minutes until golden and slightly crispy. Add a lot of sea salt to taste.
7. Serve soup with mixed mushrooms that have been sautéed on top. You can add microgreens, chili flakes, a drizzle of coconut milk, or both.

49. LENTIL KALE SOUP

Prep Time: 15 Minutes | Cook Time: 45 Minutes

Total Time: 1 Hour | Serving: 6

Ingredients

- 3 cups of chopped kale
- Olive oil
- 3 stalks celery, diced
- Salt and pepper to taste
- 3 medium carrots, peeled and diced
- ½ tsp ground cumin
- 1 tsp dried Italian seasoning

- 2 cups of dried green lentils - rinsed through a colander
- 1 (14-ounce) can diced tomatoes
- 8 cups of vegetable broth - plus more as needed
- 1 medium yellow onion, diced
- 1 tsp smoked paprika
- 4 cloves garlic, minced

Instructions

1. Heat 2 tbsp of olive oil in a big Dutch oven. You can cook the onions and celery for five to six minutes until they get soft. Add minced garlic and stir. Cook for another one to two minutes until the garlic smells good. Put cumin, paprika, Italian seasoning, salt, and pepper on top of the food to taste.
2. Please put in the diced carrots and mix them in, too.
3. Mix the diced tomatoes from the can with the lentils.
4. Add the vegetable broth and mix it in. Add pepper and salt to taste.
5. Bring to a boil, then turn down the heat so it simmers. Simmer for forty-five minutes, stirring now and then, with the lid partially covered. The lentils should be soft by then.
6. Blend the soup a few times with a KitchenAid immersion blender, but don't make it completely smooth. This is just to make it look the same. Mix ⅓ of the soup and add it back to the pot.
7. If you want the kale to get soft, add it now and cook for three more minutes. If it's too thick, you can add more broth. Make the seasonings taste better.

50. TOMATO QUINOA SOUP

Prep Time: 15 Minutes | Cook Time: 15 Minutes

Total Time: 30 Minutes | Serving: 4

Ingredients

- 2 tbsp olive oil
- ¼ cup of pumpkin seeds
- 2 cups of low-sodium vegetable broth
- 2 medium shallots, chopped
- 1 tsp minced garlic
- 2 tbsp butter or vegan butter alternative
- ½ tsp salt (or to taste), divided
- 2 28 ounce cans whole tomatoes
- 2 cups of cooked quinoa, cooked, add a pinch of salt
- ½ tsp pepper (or to taste), divided
- 1 tbsp Italian seasoning

Instructions

1. Heat butter in oil over medium heat until butter melts.
2. When you add the shallots to the pan, cook them for two to three minutes until they get soft. Put a little salt and pepper on top.
3. Mix in the garlic until it starts to smell good. Thirty seconds or so. Caution: Do not burn the garlic.
4. Put in the broth, tomatoes, and Italian seasoning. Gradually raise the heat until the water almost boils.
5. Lower the heat to medium to low and let it simmer for 15 minutes, stirring now and then.
6. The soup should be blended until smooth using a KitchenAid immersion blender.
7. Place a scoop of quinoa in the soup and top it off with pumpkin seeds. Parmesan cheese can be added if you're not a vegan.

51. CHICKPEA SOUP

Prep Time: 5 Minutes | Cook Time: 25 Minutes

Total Time: 30 Minutes | Serving: 4

Ingredients

- 1 tbsp olive oil
- 1 large lemon, juiced
- 2 cans (15 ounces) of chickpeas, drained & rinsed
- 2 large celery ribs, chopped
- ¾ tsp dried oregano
- 1 tsp salt, more to taste
- 1 tsp dried thyme
- 3 cloves garlic, minced
- 3 – 4 cups of baby spinach
- 1 small yellow onion, diced

- 1 medium zucchini, cut into half-moons
- 6 cups of low-sodium vegetable broth or chicken broth
- 2 – 3 large carrots, peeled and chopped
- ¼ cups of fresh parsley chopped
- ½ tsp black pepper
- ½ tsp crushed red pepper, optional for spice
- Optional garnishes: parsley, feta cheese, or parmesan cheese

Instructions

1. Heat 1 tbsp of olive oil over medium-high heat in a large pot or Dutch oven.
2. After you add the diced onion, cook for three to five minutes or until the onion turns clear.
3. Add the zucchini, celery, and carrots to the pan. Cook for another two to three minutes.
4. On top of that, add the crushed red pepper, salt, black pepper, dried thyme, and dried oregano. For one minute, cook until the garlic smells good.
5. Include the chickpeas and vegetable broth. After the soup starts to boil, turn down the heat to medium-low and let it cook for twenty to thirty minutes.
6. Add 1 to 2 cups of the soup (broth and chickpeas) to a blender and pulse a few times. You shouldn't add the celery or zucchini, but you can add the carrots and onions. By adding this step, the soup will naturally get thicker. Use a fork to mash 1 cup of the chickpeas if you don't have a blender. Then, add that back to the soup. You can also pulse a KitchenAid immersion blender five to ten times.
7. Put the mixed ingredients back into the pot and stir them around. Don't blend everything because you still want whole chickpeas in the soup.
8. Put in the lemon juice, chopped spinach, and fresh parsley. Add the spinach and cook for one to two more minutes until it softens.
9. Serve hot with sprinkle of fresh parsley on top. You can also put some feta cheese on top if you want to.

52. LENTIL SOUP

Prep Time: 5 Minutes | Cook Time: 40 Minutes

Total Time: 45 Minutes | Serving: 4

Ingredients

- 1 + 1/2 tsp crushed black pepper (add less for less of a kick)
- 2 cloves of garlic, minced
- 3/4 tsp cumin
- 2 cups of water
- 2 tbsp fresh lemon juice
- 2 cups of riced cauliflower; mine was frozen

- 3 cups of low-sodium veggie broth
- 2 tbsp tomato paste
- 1 tsp salt, or more to taste.
- 1 cup of dry red lentils
- 1 small white onion, chopped
- 2 tbsp olive oil
- 1 tsp garlic powder

Top With:

- Coconut milk, greek yogurt, crushed crackers

Instructions

1. Put the chopped onion in a large pot and cook it in olive oil over medium to low heat for three to four minutes. Toss everything together for one more minute when you add the minced garlic.
2. Turn the heat to medium-low and stir in the lentils, cauliflower rice, tomato paste, and spices. Do this for one to two minutes.
3. Add the water and vegetable broth to the pot. Cover it and bring it to a boil. Lower the heat to low and let the soup simmer for about 35 minutes after it starts to boil.
4. Taste the soup every 10 minutes and add more salt or pepper as needed. Add about 2 tbsp of fresh lemon juice near the end and mix it in.
5. Blending the lentils is unnecessary because they break up with the liquid. You can use your KitchenAid immersion blender or wait until the soup is cool and then blend it in your blender.
6. Add your favorite crackers or coconut milk from a can on top!

53. BROCCOLI SOUP

Prep Time: 10 Minutes | Cook Time: 25 Minutes

Total Time: 35 Minutes | Serving: 6

Ingredients

- 1 onion, chopped
- 2 cups of milk
- 5 tbsp butter, divided
- 3 tbsp all-purpose flour
- 1 stalk celery, chopped
- ground black pepper to taste
- 8 cups of broccoli floret
- 3 cups of chicken broth

Instructions

1. Gather everything you need.
2. In a medium stock pot, melt 2 tbsp of butter over medium heat. Cook the celery and onion until they are soft.
3. Cover and let it cook for 10 minutes after adding the broccoli and broth.
4. Put the soup into a KitchenAid immersion blender until the pitcher is half full. Use a folded kitchen towel to hold down the blender's lid while you carefully turn it on. Give the soup a few quick pulses to get it moving before leaving it on to puree. Blend in parts until smooth, then pour into a clean pot. You can blend the soup by putting the blender right into the pot.
5. In a small saucepan over medium to low heat, melt 3 tbsp of butter. Add the flour and milk and stir them together. Mix it until it gets thick and bubbly, then add it to the soup. Add pepper, and then serve.
6. Enjoy while hot.

54. ZUCCHINI SOUP

Prep Time: 15 Minutes | Cook Time: 30 Minutes

Total Time: 45 Minutes | Serving: 4

Ingredients

- 4 medium zucchini (1 ½ to 2 pounds)
- 2 tbsp olive oil
- 1 small onion, finely chopped
- ¼ tsp ground black pepper
- 1 tsp kosher salt
- 3 cups of vegetable or chicken broth,
- 2 tbsp fresh lemon juice
- 2 garlic cloves, minced
- ¼ cup of raw cashews
- 2 tbsp chopped fresh herbs (dplus more for garnish

Instructions

1. In a big pot, heat the oil over medium-high heat. Put in the onion and cook it for four to five minutes until it gets soft. After you add the garlic, stir for one more minute.
2. Bring the cashews, zucchini, broth, salt, and pepper to a boil. Low-level the heat, cover, and let it cook for 15 to 20 minutes or until the zucchini is soft.
3. Mix the chopped herbs with the soup and add the lemon juice. Afterward, blend the soup until smooth with a KitchenAid immersion blender (stick blender) or add small amounts at a time to a high-powered blender and blend for 20 to 30 seconds until smooth.
4. Put bowls of the zucchini soup together and top each one with fresh herbs and a drizzle of olive oil.

55. GREEN VELVET SOUP

Prep Time: 10 Minutes | Cook Time: 1 Hour 20 Minutes

Total Time: 1 Hour 30 Minutes | Serving: 8

Ingredients

- salt to taste
- 2 zucchini, diced
- 4 cups of chopped fresh spinach
- 6 cups of vegetable broth
- ¾ cup of dried split peas
- 2 bay leaves
- 2 stalks celery, sliced
- 1 onion, chopped
- 1 head of broccoli, chopped
- ½ tsp dried basil
- 2 potatoes, diced
- ¼ tsp ground black pepper

Instructions

1. Put the potatoes, split peas, onion, celery, bay leaves, and broth in a large pot over medium-low heat. Bring to a boil, then lower the heat, cover, and let it cook for one hour.
2. Take out the bay leaves and add the broccoli, zucchini, basil, and black pepper. Let it cook for 20 minutes or until the broccoli is soft.
3. Add the spinach and stir it in. Then, take it off the heat. I used a KitchenAid immersion blender to puree the food in a blender. Add salt to taste.

56. TOMATILLO SALSA VERDE

Prep Time: 5 Minutes | Cook Time: 10 Minutes | Total Time: 15 Minutes | Serving: 2

Ingredients

- 1 jalapeño use half for less spicy salsa
- ⅓ sprig of fresh cilantro stems removed
- 2 garlic cloves unpeeled
- 1 poblano chile seeded and sliced half
- 10 tomatillos de-husked and quartered
- ½ tsp sea salt
- 2 tbsp lime juice approx. 1 lime

Instructions

1. Set the broiler to high and line aluminum foil on a baking sheet.
2. Put the garlic cloves, jalapeños, poblanos, and tomatillos on the baking sheet. Do not peel the garlic cloves yet. Keep the baking sheet in the oven and broil for 8 to 10 minutes or until the garlic is nicely charred.
3. Add sea salt, fresh cilantro leaves, and lime juice in a KitchenAid immersion blender. Don't forget to peel the garlic first.Mix until it's smooth.

57. PEA KALE SOUP

Prep Time: 15 Minutes | Cook Time: 55 Minutes

Total Time: 1 Hour 10 Minutes | Serving: 4

Ingredients

Kale & Pea Soup:

- 2 cups of water
- 5 whole shallots, chopped
- 2.5 ounce spinach
- 3 cloves garlic
- 2 cups of vegetable broth
- 3 ounce cremini mushrooms, stems removed & chopped
- 1/3 cup of parsley
- 1 cup of frozen peas, thawed
- 1/4 cup of arborio rice
- 2 tbsp olive oil
- 1/8 tsp cayenne pepper
- 5 ounce kale, stems removed and chopped

Simple Cream:

- 1/8 tsp pepper
- 4 tbsp sour cream (plant-based)
- 1/8 tsp salt
- 2 tbsp water
- 1/2 whole lemon, juiced

Instructions

1. Set a Dutch oven or big pot on low heat. Put in olive oil. When the olive oil starts to shimmer, add the shallot and cook for about 20 minutes until the shallot is clear and smells good.
2. When you add the cremini mushrooms, cook for about 5 minutes or until they give off their liquid.
3. Put in the garlic, cayenne pepper, and arborio rice. Mix them.
4. Put in the peas, water, and vegetable broth. Turn up the heat to high and boil it. Turn down the heat, cover, and let it cook for 15 minutes.
5. Put in the parsley and kale. Once the greens are fully covered in liquid, mix them. Put the lid back on and cook for 10 minutes or until the greens are soft.
6. Take the pan off the heat and add the spinach. Mix it in until it starts to wilt.
7. Use an immersion blender from KitchenAid to blend until smooth.
8. Put the ingredients for simple cream in a small bowl and mix them. Serve on the side.

58. KALE POTATO LEEK SOUP

Prep Time: 30 Minutes | Cook Time: 1 Hour

Total Time: 1 Hour 30 Minutes | Serving: 6

Ingredients

- 1/2 cup of sour cream
- Kosher salt to taste
- 3 large leeks (about 1 pound), cleaned and thinly sliced
- 4-5 medium russet potatoes (about 1 pound), peeled and roughly chopped
- 1/2 cup of heavy cream
- 1 bunch kale, chopped (about 1/2 pound)
- Freshly ground pepper
- 1-2 tbsp freshly squeezed lemon juice
- 2 dried bay leaves
- 2 tbsp neutral oil, such as canola
- 6 cups of vegetable stock or chicken stock
- Bacon bits for garnish
- Finely chopped kale for garnish

Instructions

1. Heat the oil over medium heat in a large stockpot (6 quarts or more). Put in the kale, potato, and leek For about 10 to 12 minutes, stirring again and again until the vegetables have started to soften and turn a little brown. This time will vary, depending on how big the bottom of your pot is.
2. Bring to a boil after adding the vegetable stock and bay leaves. Turn down the heat and let it simmer for thirty to forty minutes or until the vegetables are soft.
3. With a KitchenAid immersion blender or by carefully moving the ingredients to a blender in batches, blend until smooth.
4. To make it taste just right, add the cream and season with lemon juice, freshly ground pepper, and salt (I start with 1 tsp and taste often).
5. Put the soup into bowls and top each with sour cream and a sprinkle of healthy kale or bacon bits.

59. GREENS AND BEANS SOUP

Prep Time: 15 Minutes | Cook Time: 10 Minutes

Total Time: 25 Minutes | Serving: 2

Ingredients

- 1 bunch organic spinach, chopped
- 4 cups of low-sodium chicken stock or vegetable broth
- 1 (15-ounce) can cannellini beans, drained
- 4 cloves garlic, chopped
- 1 bunch organic kale, chopped
- 1 tsp ground turmeric
- 1/2 tsp black pepper

- 2 large shallots, chopped
- 2 tbsp olive oil
- 1/4 tsp ground allspice
- 1/2 tsp freshly grated nutmeg
- 1 tsp salt
- 1/2 cup of fresh cilantro, chopped
- Low-fat (2%) Greek yogurt, to serve (optional)

Instructions

1. Warm up the olive oil in a big pot over medium heat. Put in the garlic and shallots. Stirring often, cook for about 5 minutes or until the vegetables are soft. Add the allspice, salt, pepper, and turmeric and mix them in. For two minutes, stir the food often. Put the stock and cannellini beans in it. Turn the heat down to low and cook for 10 minutes.
2. Put the kale, spinach, and cilantro in the pot. Skim the water over medium-low heat and cook for 10 minutes. In batches, you should move the soup to a blender or KitchenAid immersion blender. Keep the blender's lid on. Remove the lid's centerpiece and place a clean kitchen towel over the hole to let the steam out. Mix until it's smooth. Check the seasonings and make changes as needed.
3. Add a dollop of Greek yogurt and a cilantro leaf as a garnish if you want to.

60. CELERIAC PARSNIP SOUP

Prep Time: 5 Minutes | Cook Time: 40 Minutes

Total Time: 45 Minutes | Serving: 8

Ingredients

- 1 red onion finely chopped
- Salt to taste
- 1 tbsp paprika
- 1 tbsp ginger grated
- 1 1/4 pounds parsnip chopped
- 2 tbsp parsley finely chopped
- 2 cloves garlic finely chopped
- 1 13.5 ounce can of coconut milk
- 1 tbsp oil
- 1 pound celeriac/celery root weight after peeling, chopped
- 6 3/4 cups of water
- 1 tsp dried tarragon
- 1/4 tsp cayenne pepper

Instructions

1. Warm up the oil. Put in the ginger, onion, and garlic. Let it cook for a few minutes until it gets soft.
2. Put in the parsnips, celeriac, and 6 cups of water. Bring up the temperature. Turn the heat down to a high level and cook for 30 minutes or until the vegetables are soft. Take it off the heat. Blend well with a KitchenAid immersion blender.
3. Bring it back to a boil, and then add the coconut milk, the rest of the water, and the rest of the ingredients. Keep cooking on low heat for five more minutes.
4. Warm up and serve.

61. GREEN GODDESS SOUP

Prep Time: 10 Minutes | Cook Time: 40 Minutes

Total Time: 50 Minutes | Serving: 6

Ingredients

- 1 red onion, chopped
- 1 broccoli, head, broken into florets
- 1 green bell pepper, chopped
- 2 broccoli stems, chopped
- 3 handfuls spinach
- 1 tsp lemon juice
- 1 zucchini, chopped
- ½ cup of coconut milk
- 4 cups of salted vegetable broth
- ¼ cup of nutritional yeast
- 1 head garlic

Instructions

1. Warm the oven up to 375F.
2. Fill a baking sheet or cast iron pan with parchment paper. Place the broccoli stems, bell pepper, zucchini, onion, and head of broccoli on it. Add freshly cracked black pepper and nutritional yeast, then drizzle with olive oil. Remove the garlic's head's top and drizzle it with olive oil. Wrap in foil. Put both in the oven and bake for 35 minutes or until the vegetables are fully cooked.
3. Put all the listed ingredients into a pot or a high-speed KitchenAid immersion blender. Squeeze the garlic into the pot or blender, then discard the skin. Mix the ingredients by hand or with an immersion blender until you have a smooth soup. If you need to, taste and add more salt.

62. CABBAGE SOUP

Prep Time: 15 Minutes | Cook Time: 30 Minutes

Total Time: 45 Minutes | Serving: 4

Ingredients

- 1 tbsp soy sauce
- 1 tbsp bouillon paste
- 1/2 tsp ground cloves
- 1 tsp liquid smoke
- 1 can white kidney beans, drained & rinsed
- 1/2 tsp dried oregano
- 2 cans water, using the bean can
- 2 tbsp olive oil

- (optional) non-dairy milk, to think

- 1/2 tsp hot chili powder
- 300 g (about 1/2 head) cabbage
- 1/2 tsp smoked paprika
- pinch cayenne
- 2 shallots, sliced
- 3 cloves garlic, sliced
- 3 bay leaves
- 2 tbsp hot pimento paste
- salt & pepper, to taste

Instructions

1. Get everything ready before you start by chopping and preparing it.
2. Put the heavy-bottomed pan on medium heat and add the olive oil. Let it heat up for one minute.
3. Insert the garlic and shallot slices and cook for three to five minutes until the vegetables are soft. Include the hot pimento paste, bay leaves, ground cloves, hot chili powder, smoked paprika, dried oregano, and cayenne. Mix these all. Combine everything and cook for one to two minutes. Include the soy sauce.
4. Add the white kidney beans and stir them around to spread all spices. Next, add the water, bouillon paste, cabbage, salt, and pepper. Cover the pot with a lid and let the food cook for 20 to 30 minutes.
5. Add liquid smoke and stir after the cabbage is soft.
6. Carefully remove the bay leaves with a slotted spoon.
7. Use an immersion blender to blend the soup until it is smooth and creamy. If you need to, add a splash of non-dairy milk to get the consistency you want. You can strain it through a sieve if you want it smooth, but we don't usually do that.
8. With crunchy croutons, pimento paste, and black pepper on top, it's ready to eat.

63. RED CABBAGE SOUP

Prep Time: 15 Minutes | Cook Time: 35 Minutes

Total Time: 50 Minutes | Serving: 4

Ingredients

- 5 cups of vegetable stock
- 3 cloves garlic minced
- 5 cups of red cabbage roughly chopped
- pepper to taste
- 1 large potato peeled, cubed
- salt to taste
- 1 medium apple peeled, chopped
- 1 tbsp olive oil
- 1 medium red onion, roughly chopped
- 2 tsp red wine vinegar
- ¼ cup of heavy cream & more for serving

Instructions

1. Put olive oil in a spacious pot and heat it over medium-high heat. Add the garlic and onions when it gets hot for three to four minutes or until fragrant and clear.
2. Put the apple, potato, and cabbage in the pot. Stir the food and cook for 5 to 7 minutes or until the cabbage gets soft.
3. Put the red wine vinegar and vegetable stock. Add pepper and salt to taste. Once the liquid starts to boil, turn down the heat and put the lid on top of the pot. Simmer for 20 minutes.
4. Put the pot away from the heat after 20 minutes. Put in the KitchenAid immersion blender and blend the food until smooth. You could also put the soup in a regular blender. Add heavy cream and mix it in. Then, put the soup into bowls to serve. Warm up and serve.

64. SPINACH SOUP

Prep Time: 10 Minutes | Cook Time: 25 Minutes

Total Time: 35 Minutes | Serving: 4

Ingredients

- 2 tsp olive oil
- 2 cloves garlic, minced
- 1 (6-ounce) bag of baby spinach, divided
- 1/2 medium onion, finely chopped
- 2 cups of chicken or vegetable broth
- 1 medium potato, peeled and cubed
- Freshly ground black pepper, to taste
- 2 cups of fat-free milk
- Kosher salt, to taste
- 1 stalk celery, finely chopped

Instructions

1. Get the ingredients together.
2. Heat the oil in a large pot or Dutch oven. It will take 5 minutes to cook the potato, onion, celery, and garlic.
3. Put in the fat-free milk and chicken broth. Cover it and let it cook on low for 10 minutes when it starts to boil.
4. Add half the spinach, cover, and cook for another 10 minutes.
5. Let the soup cool down, then put it in a blender. Work in two batches so the hot soup doesn't fill up the blender too quickly if you need to. You can also use an immersion blender from KitchenAid to blend the soup in the pot. Blend the soup until it is smooth after adding the rest of the fresh spinach.
6. Make sure it tastes right, then serve.

65. ZUCCHINI BASIL SOUP

Prep Time: 5 Minutes | Cook Time: 15 Minutes

Total Time: 20 Minutes | Serving: 4

Ingredients

- 1 tbsp olive oil
- ⅛ tsp pepper, or more to taste
- ½ small lemon, juiced
- ½ tsp salt
- 1.5 pounds zucchini, cubed
- 1 medium onion, chopped
- 24 ounces broth, vegetable or chicken
- 3 cloves garlic, minced
- ½ cup of packed basil leaves

Instructions

5. Put olive oil in a stock pot and set it over medium heat. When it's hot, put the diced onion and cook for three to four minutes, until the onions turn brown and clear. After you add the garlic, cook for another 30 seconds. Pour in the broth and seasoning them with salt and pepper. Bring to a boil, then turn the heat low and cover. Slowly cook for 8 to 10 minutes or until the zucchini is soft and cooked.
6. Take it off the heat and add the lemon juice and basil leaves.
7. Blend until smooth with a KitchenAid immersion blender. Remove the center cap from the lid and cover it properly with a kitchen towel to let the steam escape. Do not put more than half of the hot soup into a blender.
8. If you want, you can top it with shredded cheese, croutons, pesto, or a splash of cream. Serve warm as a side dish.

66. ASPARAGUS SOUP

Prep Time: 20 Minutes | Cook Time: 55 Minutes

Total Time: 1 Hour 15 Minutes | Serving: 12

Ingredients

- 1 medium onion, chopped
- 2 pounds fresh asparagus, trimmed and cut into 1-inch pieces
- 2/3 cup of uncooked long-grain brown rice
- 1 tbsp butter
- 1/4 tsp dried thyme
- 1 tbsp olive oil
- 1 medium carrot, thinly sliced
- 6 cups of reduced-sodium chicken broth
- 1/4 tsp pepper
- 1/2 tsp salt
- Salad croutons, optional
- Reduced-fat sour cream, optional

Instructions

1. Slowly melt the butter and oil in a 6-quart stockpot. Add the vegetables and seasonings and stir them in. Cook for 10 minutes, stirring now and then, until the vegetables are soft.
2. Add the broth and rice and stir them in. Bring the mixture to a boil. Lower the heat and let the rice simmer, covered, for 40 to 45 minutes, stirring now and then.
3. You can use an immersion blender from KitchenAid to puree the soup or let it cool a bit and blend it in batches in a regular blender. Put everything back in the pot and heat it all the way through. Add sour cream and croutons if you like.

67. PEA SOUP WITH QUINOA

Prep Time: 10 Minutes | Cook Time: 25 Minutes

Total Time: 35 Minutes | Serving: 6

Ingredients

- 1/4 tsp pepper
- 2-1/2 cups of frozen peas (about 10 ounces)
- 1 medium onion, chopped
- 2 tsp canola oil
- 1/2 cup of quinoa, rinsed
- 1/2 tsp salt
- 1 cup of water
- 2 cans (14-1/2 ounces each) of reduced-sodium chicken broth or vegetable broth
- Optional toppings: Plain yogurt, croutons, shaved Parmesan cheese and cracked pepper

Instructions

1. Bring water to a boil in a small pot. Put in quinoa. Reduce the heat and let it simmer, covered, for 12 to 15 minutes or until the water is gone.
2. In the meantime, heat the oil in a large saucepan over medium-high heat. Add the onion and cook it until it's soft. Add the broth and peas and stir them in. Bring the mixture to a boil. Lowered the heat and let it simmer for about 5 minutes, or until the peas are soft.
3. Use an immersion blender from KitchenAid to blend the soup. Or, let the soup cool a bit and then blend it in a blender before putting it back in the pan. Add the quinoa, salt, and pepper, and heat it through. Put on top of your choice of toppings.

68. GREEN SOUP WITH CASHEW CREAM

Prep Time: 15 Minutes | Cook Time: 20 Minutes

Total Time: 35 Minutes | Serving: 4

Ingredients

- 3 cups of broccoli
- Lemon juice to taste
- 1 cup of edamame
- 6 cups of vegetable stock
- 1 cup of spinach
- 2 cups of frozen peas

- 4 tbsp nutritional yeast (or sub for parmesan)
- salt & pepper
- 3/4 cup of cashews soaked in water
- 1 onion chopped
- 3 cloves of garlic

Instructions

1. Put the cashews in water and let them soak for at least two hours or overnight.
2. Put the garlic and onion in butter and chop them up.
3. Put broccoli, peas, and edamame in the stock and cook until the vegetables are soft. Close the lid and wait 15 minutes. Food will cook faster with the steam.
4. While you wait, rinse the cashews and put them in a blender with 1/2 cup of water. This will make the cashew cream. Mix until it's smooth.
5. Put spinach into the soup and cook for a few minutes until it wilts. Put most cashew cream on top, but save some for the top.
6. Use an immersion blender from KitchenAid to blend soup.
7. Add more pepper and salt to taste.
8. To taste, add some lemon juice. Top it with cashew cream and parmesan or nutritional yeast to keep it vegan.

69. SPLIT PEA SOUP

Prep Time: 10 Minutes | Cook Time: 2 Hour 30 Minutes

Total Time: 2 Hour 40 Minutes | Serving: 12

Ingredients

- 8 cups of boiling water
- 1 large onion (chopped)
- 3 carrots (chopped)
- 3 celery stalks (chopped)
- 2 tbsp olive oil
- 1/2 tsp dried basil
- 1/2 tsp dried thyme
- 3 bay leaves
- 3 cloves garlic (chopped)
- 1 1/2 tsp salt
- 2 cups of dried split peas
- 1/2 tsp fresh parsley (chopped)
- 1 potato, peeled and chopped (optional)

Instructions

1. Warm up the oil in a big soup pot over medium-low heat. Add the garlic, bay leaf, onion, celery, and carrots, and cook them until the onions become clear.
2. Put in the salt, water, and peas.
3. Turn down the heat, boil for a minute, then let it cook for another hour and a half.
4. Put in the pepper, spinach, basil, thyme, and potato. Put the lid on and cook on low heat for an hour until the vegetables and peas are soft enough to mash.
5. Blend the soup until it's smooth with a KitchenAid immersion blender.

70. PEA, MINT & COCONUT SOUP

Prep Time: 10 Minutes | Cook Time: 15 Minutes

Total Time: 25 Minutes | Serving: 4

Ingredients

- 1,5 cup of vegetable broth or water
- 500 g shelled peas, about 1,5 kilos with pods (or thawed frozen peas)
- 2 cloves garlic
- 1 tbsp coconut oil, ghee, or cold-pressed olive oil
- 10 sprigs fresh mint
- 1 onion
- 1,5 cup of full-fat coconut milk
- 1 tsp sea salt
- cold-pressed olive oil for serving
- purple micro greens (or pea sprouts) for serving

Instructions

1. Cut the garlic cloves and onion into large pieces.
2. In a saucepan, heat the coconut oil over medium-low heat. Put in the garlic and onions. Cook for three to five minutes until soft but not browned.
3. Put the peas, salt, mint, and coconut milk in the water or vegetable broth. Bring to a very low simmer. Take the heat off.
4. Use an immersion blender from KitchenAid to blend until smooth. If needed, add more water. Add salt and pepper to taste.
5. Sprinkle with microgreens, salt, and pepper, and serve in bowls.
6. It stays good in the fridge for three to five days.

71. SMOKEY BLACK BEAN SOUP

Prep Time: 5 Minutes | Cook Time: 30 Minutes

Total Time: 35 Minutes | Serving: 4

Ingredients

- 1 tbsp smoked paprika
- 1 tbsp Worcestershire sauce
- 1/2 tsp chipotle powder
- 3 15-ounce cans black beans, drained & rinsed
- 2 tsp. ground cumin
- 4 cups of low-sodium vegetable broth

- 2 tbsp avocado oil
- 1 14.5-ounce can of fire-roasted diced tomatoes
- 1 1/2 tsp kosher salt
- 4-6 cloves garlic, peeled, minced
- 1/2 tsp ground black pepper
- 1 medium red onion, diced
- 1/2 tsp dried oregano

For serving:

- Plain unsweetened Greek yogurt or sour Cream
- Chopped cilantro

- Tortilla chips
- Diced avocado

Instructions

1. Warm up the avocado oil in a big pot with a heavy bottom, like a Dutch oven. Add the diced red onion after 7 or 8 minutes and continue cooking until the onion becomes transparent.
2. After a minute or two, stir in the minced garlic.
3. Add the spices and cook for 45 to 60 seconds until the spices start to smell good.
4. Add the diced tomatoes and stir. Make sure to scrape the bottom of the pot to get rid of any stuck bits.
5. Put in the Worcestershire sauce, vegetable broth, and black beans. Mix them all together in the pot. Put a lid on it and boil it.
6. Turn the heat to medium-low, and leave the soup alone for 20 minutes.
7. Take the pot off the heat and blend some soup with a KitchenAid immersion blender. (You can make it very smooth or leave it with some chunks; it's up to you!) If you don't have a KitchenAid immersion blender, you may use a regular blender to make about 2 cups of the soup smooth. Then, add that to the pot with the rest of the soup.
8. Add tortilla chips, diced avocado, chopped cilantro, and plain Greek yogurt on top immediately to serve.

72. CARROT AND GINGER SOUP

Prep Time: 10 Minutes | Cook Time: 45 Minutes

Total Time: 55 Minutes | Serving: 4

Ingredient

- 2 tbsp olive oil
- ½ medium butternut squash
- 1 pinch ground cinnamon
- 3 cloves garlic, crushed or to taste
- 1 (2 inch) piece fresh ginger, peeled & thinly sliced
- 1 pound carrots - peeled and diced
- salt and pepper to taste
- 1 onion, diced
- 4 cups of water
- ¼ cup of heavy cream (Optional)

Instructions

1. Turn the oven on to 350 degrees F (175 degrees C). Take the butternut squash half in half and scoop out the seeds. Then, put the cut side down on a greased baking sheet. For 30 to 40 minutes, or until soft, bake. Scoop out its flesh with a large spoon once the squash has cooled. Set aside.
2. In a large pot, heat the olive oil over medium-low heat. Put in the chopped onion and garlic. Stir the food while cooking until the onion turns clear. Add the water and then the squash, carrots, and ginger. Wait at least 20 minutes, or until the carrots and ginger are soft after you bring it to a boil.
3. Mix it all together with the KitchenAid immersion blender. Don't forget that this is supposed to be a thick, creamy soup. If you need to thin it out, add boiling water. Put the soup back in the pan and heat it through. Add cinnamon, salt, and pepper to taste.
4. Pour into bowls for serving. You can add a garnish of a thin swirl of Cream on top if you want.

73. CARROT AND CORIANDER SOUP

Prep Time: 10 Minutes | Cook Time: 20 Minutes

Total Time: 30 Minutes | Serving: 4

Ingredients

- 1 garlic clove, peeled and sliced
- 1 tbsp olive oil, extra virgin
- 800 g carrots, peeled and cut into rounds
- 10 g fresh coriander leaves and stalks
- ½ tsp ground coriander
- 1 red onion, peeled and diced
- 750 ml chicken stock or vegetable stock

Instructions

1. In a pan over medium heat, cook the onion and garlic, stirring often, until the onion is clear. It takes about 5 minutes to do this.
2. Blend the coriander into a powder and stir it in for 30 seconds.
3. Put the chicken stock and carrots in the pan. Bring it to a boil, then cook on low for 15 minutes until the carrots are soft. Cover the pan only partially and stir it now and then.
4. Wait 15 minutes after cooking the carrots before eating them. After putting everything in a blender, add the fresh coriander and blend until it's smooth. Depending on your blender's size, you might have to do this in several steps. You can also use a KitchenAid stick blender or immersion blender.
5. Keep the soup back in the pan and heat it before serving it. Add salt and pepper to taste. Add some extra coriander leaves, and serve with warm, crusty bread.

74. ROASTED PUMPKIN APPLE SOUP

Prep Time: 10 Minutes | Cook Time: 40 Minutes

Total Time: 50 Minutes | Serving: 6

Ingredients

- Black pepper
- 1 cup of light coconut milk
- Salt
- 2 apples - washed, cored, and quartered (leave the skin on)
- 1 carrot - peeled and cut into chunks
- 1 onion - skin removed and chopped
- Pumpkin (about 500 g)
- 2 bay leaves
- 2 cups of water
- 3 - 4 shakes of smoked paprika
- 2 tbsp olive oil (divided)

Garnish:

- Black pepper
- Pumpkin seeds

Instructions

1. Clean the pumpkin and take out the seeds. Take off the pumpkin's skin and cut it up. You could also leave the skin on the pumpkin and take out the flesh later. Line a baking sheet using parchment paper with pumpkin pieces, onions, apples, and carrots. Add salt and drizzle with 1 tbsp of olive oil.
2. Warm the oven up to 180 degrees C. Put the pumpkin and carrots in the oven for 30 minutes until they are soft and the edges are light brown.
3. In a medium-sized deep pot, heat 1 tbsp of olive oil. Cook onions until they are soft and clear. Return the roasted foods, paprika, and bay leaves to the pot. Sauté for one more minute.
4. Put water in. Bring it to a boil, then cook it on low for five minutes. Add salt and pepper to taste.
5. Take out the bay leaves. Blend the soup until it's smooth with a KitchenAid immersion blender. Add a little water to thin out the soup if you think it's too thick.
6. Fill bowls with food. Add your favorite toppings on top. Some ideas for toppings are chili, black pepper, chopped coriander, Cream, pumpkin seeds, and so on.

75. POTATO WITH ROSEMARY SOUP

Prep Time: 15 Minutes | Cook Time: 30 Minutes

Total Time: 45 Minutes | Serving: 8

Ingredients

- 1 ½ cups of half-and-half (or whole milk)
- 3 large garlic cloves, thickly sliced
- 3 cups of chicken broth, homemade or from a carton or can
- 2 tbsp olive oil
- 1 ½ tsp minced fresh rosemary
- 1 large onion, cut into large dice
- Salt and freshly ground pepper to taste
- ⅛ tsp cayenne pepper
- 1 pinch sugar
- 1 ½ pounds peeled russet (Idaho) potatoes, cut into 1-inch chunks
- 1 tbsp butter
- Garnish: crumbled bacon

Instructions

1. Heat the oil over medium-high heat in a big, deep sauté pan until it shimmers.
2. First, add the potatoes, then the onion. Sauté, stirring very little at first, then more often, for 7 to 8 minutes or until the squash turns golden brown.
3. Turn down the heat and add the butter, sugar, and garlic. Keep cooking for another 10 minutes or until all the vegetables are a rich, spotty caramel color.
4. Add the cayenne pepper and cook again for 30 seconds to a minute until the food smells good.
5. Add the broth and heat it to a medium-high level. Lower the heat to low and let the potatoes cook for about 10 minutes with the lid partially on top.
6. Add fresh rosemary to the KitchenAid immersion blender and puree until very smooth, for 30 seconds to a minute. Place a kitchen towel over the blender's container. Pour a little half-and-half into the canister to "clean" it. Blend it for a short time, then add it to the soup.
7. Put it back in the pan or soup pot and add half-and-half until it's soup-like but thick enough to float the garnish. Add salt and pepper if needed. Bring to a boil, pour into bowls, decorate, and serve.

76. CARROT GINGER SOUP

Prep Time: 10 Minutes | Cook Time: 20 Minutes

Total Time: 30 Minutes | Serving: 4

Ingredients

- 1 tsp Sriracha
- 3 cups of vegetable broth
- 2 tbsp olive oil
- 2" fresh ginger
- salt and pepper
- 1 yellow onion
- 4 cloves garlic
- 7 carrots, medium
- 1 can of coconut milk

Instructions

1. Put the Instant Pot on sauté and cut the onions into small pieces. For three to four minutes, cook on some olive oil.
2. Take the carrots and cut them up. Then, add them to the onions. Cut the garlic into small pieces and peel and mince the ginger. Put it on top of the carrots. Add Sriracha, vegetable broth, and salt and pepper to taste.
3. Put the lid back on the Instant Pot and cover the vent. After 10 minutes of high-pressure cooking, let the pressure out and use an immersion blender from KitchenAid to blend.
4. Mix the coconut milk in well, then serve.

77. ONION SOUP

Prep Time: 25 Minutes | Cook Time: 45 Minutes

Total Time: 1 Hour 5 Minutes | Serving: 8

Ingredients

- Salt and pepper
- 1 Bouquet Garni, a small fresh herb bouquet with thyme and a bay leaf
- 1 tbsp balsamic vinegar
- 1 sheet frozen puff pastry, thawed
- 5 tbsp butter
- 1 cup of shredded Fontina cheese
- 6 cups of water
- 1 tbsp honey
- 1/3-1/2 cup of Heavy Cream
- 2 cups of dry white wine
- 2 tbsp Beef Base Paste + 1 teaspoon
- 1 large Russet potato, peeled and chopped
- 3 pounds onions, peeled and roughly chopped
- 3 cloves garlic, peeled and chopped

Instructions

1. Put the onions, potato, and garlic in a large saucepan with butter. Cook over medium-low heat until the onions are soft and brown, almost burned. The whole thing could take more than 30 minutes. About 15 minutes in, add 1 tbsp of honey to help it caramelize. If necessary, turn down the heat.
2. Use 2 cups of wine to clear the pan. After that, put in the water, beef base, and bouquet garni. After 15 minutes, take out the bouquet garni and blend the soup with a KitchenAid immersion blender. Add the Cream and balsamic vinegar and mix well. After all , add salt and pepper to taste.
3. In the meantime, heat the oven to 400 degrees F and put parchment paper on a baking sheet. Cut out 8 or more circles the size of your serving cups of with a cookie cutter or a glass.
4. After putting the puff pastry rounds in the oven for 15 minutes, sprinkle them with Fontina cheese. They should be lightly golden and fluffy. Put a cheese pillow on top of each cup of soup to serve.

78. CARROT MISO SOUP

Prep Time: 5 Minutes | Cook Time: 25 Minutes

Total Time: 30 Minutes | Serving: 3

Ingredients

- scallions or chives, thinly sliced
- 2 – 2 1/2 lbs. carrots, peeled & chopped
- 1/4 cup of (4 tablespoons) white miso paste
- 4 garlic cloves, minced
- 1 large onion, diced
- 4 cups of water or vegetable broth
- 1 tbsp sesame oil or 1/4 cup of water
- 1 1/2 tbsp fresh ginger, well grated
- cayenne pepper as a garnish, to taste
- 2 – 4 oz. organic silken tofu, thin sliced 1-inch pieces (optional)

Instructions

1. Heat oil in a Dutch oven over medium-low heat. Add the onion, carrots, and sauté for 5 minutes or until the carrots are clear. Then, Pour the garlic and ginger and cook for one more minute.
2. Take the mixture to a boil, then cover, lower the heat, and let it simmer for 20 minutes, stirring now and then until the carrots are soft.
3. Take a break and let the soup cool down. You can add miso to soup and puree it in one of three ways: A KitchenAid blender that fits right in the pot. You might need to puree the last two methods in groups.
4. Finishing: If you need to, add a little more water. You may want to add salt if you didn't use vegetable stock and want to make the dish taste better. Feel free to add more miso, ginger, or pepper to your liking.
5. Place bowls of soup on a serving tray. Add sliced tofu, cayenne pepper for heat, and chives or scallions on top. Have fun!

79. CARROT SOUP

Prep Time: 10 Minutes | Cook Time: 30 Minutes

Total Time: 40 Minutes | Serving: 8

Ingredients

- 4 cups of Vegetable Stock
- 2 tsp Thai Red Curry Paste
- 1 cup of Heavy Cream
- 1 tbsp Olive Oil
- 2 ½ Pounds Carrots Sliced
- Salt and Pepper To Taste
- 1 Medium Onion White, Yellow or Brown, well Chopped
- 1 tsp Crushed Garlic

For Serving (Optional):

- Ground Black Pepper
- Chopped Parsley
- Heavy Cream For swirling

Instructions

1. Put chopped onion, crushed garlic, and Thai red curry paste in a pot with olive oil. Sauté until the onions get soft.
2. Bring the vegetable stock and chopped carrots to a boil. Lower the heat, cover the pot, and let it simmer. Keep an eye on it and cook the carrots until they are soft.
3. Blend the soup in the pot using a KitchenAid immersion blender for best results. If you don't have one, carefully transfer the soup to your blender jug and blend it in stages. Once it's all smooth, return it to the pot.
4. Mix in the Cream.
5. You can add salt and pepper after the taste test.
6. Serve with a swirl of Cream, black pepper, and chopped parsley on top to look nice.

80. ROSEMARY-POTATO SOUP

Prep Time: 30 Minutes | Cook Time: 4 Hour

Total Time: 4 Hour 30 Minutes | Serving: 5

Ingredients

- ½ cup of heavy cream or half-and-half
- ¾ cup of plain full-fat Greek yogurt, room temperature
- 3 tbsp cornstarch
- 3 sprigs fresh rosemary
- 1.5 lbs Yukon gold potatoes
- 4 garlic cloves, minced
- ⅓ cup of grated Parmigiano-Reggiano cheese
- 1 yellow onion, finely chopped
- 4 cups of small cauliflower florets
- ¾ tsp cracked black pepper
- 1 cup of grated sharp white cheddar cheese
- 3 to 4 cups of vegetable broth
- 1 tsp kosher salt
- Add crumbled bacon or crispy pancetta and finely chopped fresh rosemary for a tasty topping.

Instructions

1. Put onion, potatoes, cauliflower, rosemary, garlic, salt, and pepper in a slow cooker. Add 3 ¼ cups of broth as well. (The vegetables only need enough broth to cover them.)
2. Let the potatoes and cauliflower cook on HIGH for 4 hours or LOW for 8 hours until soft enough to pierce with a fork.
3. Take out the rosemary sprigs, which should be almost empty. Blend about a third of the soup with a KitchenAid immersion blender. You could also use a potato masher to break up some cauliflower and potatoes.
4. Add cornstarch to heavy Cream or half-and-half in a liquid measuring cup. Stir until there are no more clumps.
5. Add the cheese, Parmesan, and Greek yogurt to the soup after adding the cream mixture. After that, cook on HIGH for 20 to 30 minutes until the cheese melts and the soup thickens.
6. Add the last ¾ cup of broth if you want a thinner consistency. Put soup into bowls and top with any toppings you like.

81. SWEET POTATO AND CRAB SOUP

Prep Time: 15 Minutes | Cook Time: 35 Minutes

Total Time: 50 Minutes | Serving: 8

Ingredients

- 2 cups of heavy whipping cream
- 1/2 tsp ground cinnamon
- 1/2 tsp cayenne pepper
- 12 ounces lump crabmeat, drained
- 1 tsp salt, divided
- 4 tsp fresh thyme leaves, divided
- 4 tbsp butter, divided
- 3 garlic cloves, minced
- 5 cups of vegetable stock
- 2 medium leeks (white portion), chopped
- 4 cups of cubed peeled sweet potatoes
- Croutons, optional

Instructions

1. Over medium heat, melt 2 tbsp butter in a Dutch oven. Put the leeks and garlic and cook for 4–6 minutes until soft.
2. Add cinnamon, cayenne, 3/4 tsp salt, and stock. Stir and boil everything. Lower the heat and cover the potatoes for 20 minutes to soften.
3. Blend the soup with a KitchenAid immersion blender or let it cool and puree in batches. Put the soup back in the pan. Add cream and 2 tsp thyme. Mix well and boil. Lower the heat and simmer for 5 to 6 minutes without the lid.
4. Meanwhile, melt the last 2 tbsp of butter in a large skillet over medium-low heat. Toss in the crab and the rest of the salt and thyme. Cook for 5 minutes, stirring gently to mix everything. Add crab mixture and croutons to each serving if you'd like.

82. THAI SEAFOOD CURRY SOUP

Prep Time: 15 Minutes | Cook Time: 30 Minutes

Total Time: 45 Minutes | Serving: 4

Ingredients

- 1/4 cup of small raw shrimp
- Other seafood that works: scallops, clams, mussels and salmon
- 1/4 cup of basil, chopped
- 1 can unsweetened coconut milk
- 1 bunch cilantro, divided
- 1/2 pound mushrooms, crimini or shiitake, sliced
- 2 jars of clam juice
- 1 lime, zest and juice
- 1/4 cup of squid, tubes, and tentacles
- 1 tbsp fish sauce
- 1 small onion, sliced thin
- 3 garlic cloves, minced
- 1 serrano chili, halved
- 2 cups of chicken/fish stock
- 1 jar red curry paste
- 1/4 cup of cod, chopped into bite-sized pieces
- 1 inch fresh ginger, minced

Instructions

1. Slowly cook the first three ingredients in some oil until they are barely soft. Then add the curry sauce, coconut milk, stock, and clam juice. Add half of the soup's cilantro, spearmint, zest, fish sauce, and lime juice. Don't forget to include the stems.
2. Bring to a boil, lower the heat, and let it cook for 20 minutes. In a different pan, cook the mushrooms until they turn golden brown.
3. Mix the soup (with added serrano and cilantro) with an immersion blender from KitchenAid until it is completely smooth and silky.
4. Add the mushrooms, basil, the rest of the cilantro leaves, and all the seafood to the broth. One more seven minutes of cooking will finish cooking all the seafood.
5. Add one more tbsp of fish sauce to the broth to season it until it tastes great. You can serve it by itself or with rice. Yum!

83. SALMON CHOWDER - LOW CARB

Prep Time: 20 Minutes | Cook Time: 20 Minutes

Total Time: 40 Minutes | Serving: 4

Ingredients

- 2½ cups of cauliflower cut into 1" pieces (mostly flowerets)
- 4 ounce - ⅓ less fat cream cheese
- 2 tsp Better Than Bouillon Chicken Base
- 1 - 1½ cups of frozen baby peas thawed
- 2 tsp Old Bay seasoning
- 8 green onions, chopped
- 1 tsp dill weed
- 4 ribs of Celery, chopped fine

- 2 tbsp butter
- 2 tsp Morton Light Salt
- 1 tsp black Pepper
- 2 tbsp gluten-purpose flour
- 1 tbsp minced Garlic
- 1 tbsp water
- 2 cups of 2% milk
- 2 cups of good chicken stock
- 8-10 oz. Fresh skinless salmon, cut into 1" chunks

Instructions

1. Put the salmon chunks aside and season them with Old Bay Seasoning.
2. Put the cauliflower and water in a bowl that can go in the microwave. Cover the bowl. For 4 to 5 minutes, heat in the microwave until soft. Put away.

Next:

1. Put the Celery and green onions in a large Dutch oven and melt the butter for three minutes or until soft, cook. Put in the Garlic and cook for one more minute.
2. Mix in the flour with a whisk, then cook for one minute while you add the milk, chicken stock, and base. Add the salt, Pepper, and dill weed as it gets thicker. For eight minutes, stir the food often.
3. Put one cup of the liquid from the pot into a large bowl. Put in the cream cheese and ½ of the cooked cauliflower. Blend until smooth with your KitchenAid immersion blender. Add the mixture to the soup pot and mix it with a whisk.
4. Add the salmon, peas, and cauliflower to the chowder and stir it in slowly off the heat. Set it aside for 5 minutes and stir it occasionally while the salmon cooks. As needed, change the seasonings.
5. Put celery leaves on top to serve.
6. Have fun!

84. CRAB SOUP

Prep Time: 15 Minutes | Cook Time: 40 Minutes

Total Time: 55 Minutes | Serving: 8

Ingredients

- 1 tsp Worcestershire Sauce
- 2 Bay Leaves
- 6 Cups of Seafood Stock
- 1-½ Cups of Dry White Wine
- Salt and Pepper to taste
- 4 Cloves Garlic chopped
- 2 tsp Old Bay Seasoning
- 5 tbsp unsalted butter

- 1 Cup of Heavy Cream
- 4-½ tbsp All Purpose Flour
- 2 tbsp Tomato Paste
- 2-½ pound Crab Meat cooked
- 3 Stalks Celery
- chopped
- 1 Large Onion chopped
- Fresh Parsley chopped for garnish

Instructions

1. Put the butter in a big pot with a heavy bottom. I like to use a Dutch oven.
2. Over medium-high heat, add the chopped onion and Celery and cook until the onions are clear.
3. Put in the tomato paste, salt, Pepper, Old Bay Seasoning, and chopped Garlic. Mix everything well.
4. Turn off the heat and stir in the flour. Cook for two minutes.
5. Bring the white wine, bay leaves, and seafood stock to a boil. Lessen the heat and let it cook slowly for forty minutes.
6. Remove the bay leaves and use a KitchenAid immersion blender to make it creamy.
7. Mix well after adding the heavy cream.
8. Add about ¾ of the crab meat to the soup, then turn off the heat.
9. Spread crab meat and chopped Parsley on the soup in bowls to serve.

85. SHRIMP BISQUE

Prep Time: 20 Minutes | Cook Time: 1 Hour

Total Time: 1 Hour 20 Minutes | Serving: 4

Ingredients

- 1 rib celery finely diced
- 4 tbsp butter divided
- ¼ tsp each salt & pepper more to taste
- 3 cups of seafood broth or chicken broth
- ¼ tsp dried thyme leaves
- 1 bay leaf
- 1 small onion chopped
- ½ cup of dry white wine
- 2 cloves Garlic minced
- 1 pound large shrimp with shells
- 1 ½ cups of half-and-half or 1 cup of heavy cream
- 3 tbsp tomato paste
- 1 small carrot diced
- chives chopped, for garnish

Instructions

1. Take the shrimp's shells off and set them aside.
2. Put one tbsp of butter in a medium-sized saucepan and set it over medium-low heat. For three to four minutes, or until done, add the shrimp. Put the shrimp in a bowl.
3. Put the white wine in the pot and cook for two minutes. Cover and turn off the heat after 5 minutes. Add the shrimp shells, bay leaf, and broth. Heat until it starts to simmer. Give it 15 minutes to rest. Strain the broth and set it aside.
4. At the same time, melt 3 tbsp of butter over medium heat in a medium-sized saucepan. It will take about 5 to 7 minutes to cook after adding the onions, Celery, and carrot until soft but not brown. After you add the Garlic, cook for one more minute.
5. Add the tomato paste, shrimp broth, thyme leaves, salt, and Pepper to taste. Simmer for 25 minutes with the lid off or until the sauce thickens.
6. Blend the soup with an immersion blender from KitchenAid until it is smooth. Add the cream and cook again for 5 minutes.
7. Cut the shrimp up very small and add it to the bisque. Add chopped chives as a garnish if you want.

86. SPICY BUTTER BEAN SOUP WITH JERK SHRIMP

Prep Time: 20 Minutes | Cook Time: 20 Minutes

Total Time: 40 Minutes | Serving: 4

Ingredients

- 3 cups of vegetable stock
- 1 tsp garlic powder
- 2 cloves garlic, chopped
- 1/2 tsp chili flakes
- 1 can goya butter beans
- Salt and Pepper to taste
- 6 sun-dried tomatoes, chopped
- 1 tsp dried thyme leaves
- 1/2 cup of chopped onion
- 2 tbsp olive oil

Instructions

1. Slowly heat the olive oil in a large pot.
2. Put in the onions and Garlic, and cook until they become clear.
3. Put in the tomatoes and chili flakes, and cook them.
4. Make a stir and add the butter beans.
5. Bring it to a boil, then add the stock, garlic powder, and thyme leaves.
6. Using short bursts, pour liquid into a blender and blend until smooth. BE WATCHFUL. Cover the blender with a towel to keep everyone safe. You can also use an immersion blender from KitchenAid.
7. Put the soup back on the stove and cook it on low for 5 minutes.
8. If you need to, add salt and Pepper.
9. Do it.

87. SMOKED SALMON CHOWDER

Prep Time: 10 Minutes | Cook Time: 20 Minutes

Total Time: 30 Minutes | Serving: 8

Ingredients

- 2 cloves Garlic minced
- 1 tsp Black Pepper
- 2 Carrots diced small
- 2 Bay Leaves
- 4 cups of Chicken Stock
- 8 oz. Hot Smoked Salmon
- 1 cup of Whole Milk or half and half
- 1.5 cups of Red Potatoes quarter size pieces; skin can stay on

- 1 tsp Dried Thyme
- 1 tsp Salt
- 1 small Yellow Onion diced small
- 2 small Leeks
- 5 slices Bacon diced small
- 2 Celery Stalks diced small
- Fresh Dill Optional Garnish

Instructions

1. Put the chopped Bacon in a big pot and cook it over medium-low heat until it gets crispy. Don't remove all the bacon bits from the pot; leave a few in there to add flavor.
2. Dice the onion, carrots, Celery, leeks, and Garlic, and add them to the pot with the Bacon. Sauté them until they become clear. Five to six minutes. Then, add the potato chips and mix them in.
3. Add the dried thyme and bay leaves after adding the chicken or vegetable broth. Turn down the heat and let the mixture simmer for a while. It usually takes about 15 to 20 minutes to cook until the vegetables are soft.
4. Take out the bay leaves and blend some of the soup with an immersion blender from KitchenAid, but leave some chunks for texture. You can move some of the soup to a blender, puree it, and then add it back to the pot if you don't have an immersion blender.
5. Incorporate the heavy cream and smoked salmon flake into the mixture. Let it cook for another 5 to 10 minutes until the salmon is fully heated.
6. Feel free to add more salt and Pepper to your liking.
7. Add chopped fresh dill, green onions, and the crispy bacon bits you saved to the top of the hot smoked salmon chowder.